Only a Mother Could Love Him

Ben Polis

Only a Mother Could Love Him

How I Lived With and Triumphed Over ADHD

HODDER
MOBIUS

Copyright © 2001 by Benjamin Polis
Preface copyright © 2004 by Edward M. Hallowell, M.D.

Originally published in Australia by Seaview Press, Henley Beach, in
2001

Revised edition published in 2005 by The Random House Publishing
Group

This edition published in 2005 by Hodder and Stoughton
A division of Hodder Headline

A Mobius Book

1

A CIP catalogue record for this title is available from the British
Library

ISBN 0 340 83892 2

Book design by Laurie Jewell
Printed and bound by Mackays of Chatham, Kent

Hodder Headline's policy is to use papers that are natural, renewable
and recyclable products and made from wood grown in sustainable
forests. The logging and manufacturing processes are expected to
conform to the environmental regulations of the country of origin.

Hodder and Stoughton
A division of Hodder Headline
338 Euston Road
London NW1 3BH

This book is dedicated

to my parents, for without them

I would have achieved little.

Acknowledgments

I would like to thank the following people who helped me with this book and had an impact on my life.

Gaye Polis, for being the best mum in the world. I have made it this far, Mum, and I owe a lot to you for my success. You were always there for me when I needed you most. Thanks for the thousands of books you posted for me over the past few years, I couldn't have done it without you, because I was still in bed! But the reason why I love you so much is because you were the only person who ever believed in me, in anything that I did, especially my book. Mum, we finally did it! Who would have thought that we would be published around the world? Only you and I! I love you, Mum! And, yes, the book was your idea, not mine!

Henry Polis, for being a great dad. We may not see eye to eye on a lot of things, but I respect you and love you dearly. If I grow up to be half the man you are, I will be a great man. I love you, too, Dad!

Adelaide Polis: We have never been good friends, for obvious reasons, but you will always be my favorite and only sister. In the future, I hope we can settle our differences and become close friends as brother and sister.

Tess Polis (my dog): You have spent many hours with me while I wrote this book. You never complained when the stereo was up loud or when it was too late at night and you wanted to go to sleep. You never complained when I was in a bad mood and were always ready for a hug. As my mother would say, "Teeeeessssssss!"

Anne Sandilands: What can I say, Grandma? You got me out of a little pickle and I will remember that for the rest of my life. Not many people would have done that for their grandson. I love you, Nana—I mean, Grandma. I know how much you hate being called *Nana.* . . .

Aunty Anne Scott: I have always seen you as a second mother to me. You have helped me on so many occasions, I could never list them all. Thank you for helping me get into university!

Uncle Phillip Scott: For taking me to my first Australian Rules Football match and for our countless hours of conversation on sports. I admire and look up to you as both a friend and an uncle.

Uncle Campbell Boak: I may not have agreed with your choice in football teams, but I agree with a lot of other people's opinion of you. You were a great man, a gentle giant, and I miss you. I think about you all the time! If I ever needed to talk, you were always there to listen. So many times you caught me doing naughty things on the trains, but you never told anyone. You always stuck up for me when other people didn't. Thank you for the great memories. I love you, Uncle Campbell!

My primary two teacher: I have very fond memories of you even though many years have passed. You were the one who recognized that I had reading problems and helped me learn to read. Without you, I may still be spelling "of" as "ov."

My principal in primary one to three: You recognized that I was a little bit different and not like everyone else, but you never held that against me.

My third year teacher: Miss D., you stuck up for me when other people wanted to expel me from school (again). You went to bat for me over and over, and I never really understood until I wrote this book that without you, I might not have come this far. Thank you!

My fourth year teacher: Mr. S., you always pointed me in the right direction, sometimes pushing me against my will. In the letter you gave me on the last day of school in the fourth year, you told me to "never sell yourself short." I hope I have not sold myself short and disappointed a man I respect so much. Here is rap for your resume: You're the greatest teacher in the whole world, and a true friend.

My principal in fourth year: Brother A., you always knew what the boys were up to, especially me. I respect you for what you have done for me, but more important, for touching all the boys' lives every day, by being their teacher and friend.

Sixth year, Mrs. N: You taught me that you can push only so hard before something breaks. You are a great person and a great teacher. We nearly made it!

Sixth year, Mr. K: Thank you for teaching me that there are some teachers out there who have mastered the art of capturing the elusive concentration of an ADHD student. I always left your class with a smile and a sense of time well spent. Your sometimes different teaching styles really captured and fueled my thirst and love for economics. I learned much more than economic principles from you. You taught me that if you make any topic fun and exciting, you can really reach students. You are one of the best teachers I have ever experienced. More important than that, you are a caring and kind man, and you do not receive the praise you deserve.

Sixth year, Mrs. A: What can I say? You are a lovely woman and a great teacher. Who would have thought that religious studies would be one of my best subjects? I hope you enjoyed our theological arguments.

Dr. Luk, you have been my psychiatrist since I was twelve. You have helped me understand myself more than anyone and have helped me through the bad times to the present good times. You are a man to be admired. You love your work but don't do it for praise. I have never met anyone like you before, and I've never met a doctor who cares as much as you do. You are a very special person.

Spencer McArtney, you may be only eight years old, but I see myself in you every day. We have had some great times together. You brighten up my day, even when you barge into my room while I am sleeping. You don't even realize it, but you helped with this book. You are a great kid and a great friend.

Contents

Preface

What would you think of a little boy who beat another child with a broomstick, exposed his private parts to his kindergarten class, shot a spear onto power lines and blew up the electrical circuits of a camp ground, went to school dressed up in metal armor, never read books from cover to cover, got into more trouble than any ten boys usually do, disregarded most rules and the people who enforce them, was a freak (according to his sister), and set many teachers' teeth on edge at the mere mention of his name?

Let me tell you what I think of him: He is a hero. I have never met Ben Polis, but I have read the unflinching account of his growing-up years that is this unique and exuberant book, a tale from Australia in which one good guy (Ben) gets labeled "bad guy" by many clueless guys (and gals) who don't get what he is about and know only what they want him to be and do.

Ben is a hero in my eyes because he does not cow-tow to the narrow demands of society, nor does he give up his love of life, the life he knows and lives. Reading his saga, I found myself cheering as he ignored a finger-wagging primary school teacher and left her spitting mad as he foiled her attempts to break his spirit. I howled with laughter as I read how he got even with another teacher who had driven him to thoughts of suicide in primary five. I beamed with joy as I read of his eventual victory when he hit his stride at the university.

Ben has attention deficit hyperactivity disorder, or ADHD. His account of growing up with this condition is spellbinding, as well as immensely useful in its practical advice.

It offers a window into the world of ADHD as vividly as any account I have ever read. Read this book and you will see that ADHD is not so much a disorder as a conglomeration of symptoms—some powerfully positive, others disruptive and difficult to manage, but all containing within them the germ of an ultimate joy of life and purposefulness.

But this is much more than a book of advice, or a book about ADHD. It is a book about how spunk can conquer superior force; how humor can prevail against those who will not laugh; how creativity trumps conventionality sooner or later; and how a team that works together can overcome any obstacle.

The reason I love Ben Polis and his team, his whiz-bang band of a family and the select enlightened teachers and other adults who saw the best in him and helped bring it out, is that they beat the big odds. It's easy to love kids who do everything right and never cause problems. But the ones who stand out as difficult, impulsive, wayward, or just plain bad are the ones who change the world—if only we don't destroy them before they get the chance.

Thanks to his mum, dad, various uncles and aunties, teachers, a doctor, and even a dog, Ben rose up and beat the Goliath of the conventional, one-size-fits-all world that children confront in school. He took his little pebble and nailed the hairy monster right between the eyes.

He won. He is winning still. Read this book and let him tell you how.

—DR. EDWARD M. HALLOWELL, M.D.

Introduction

When I was seventeen, my psychiatrist suggested that I write a book on my personal experiences of suffering from attention deficit hyperactivity disorder (ADHD). I did not give the idea a second thought. The answer was a plain and simple "No!" I did not want to talk about it. I didn't even want to think about my personal experiences with ADHD.

I was sick and tired of always being looked upon as that "crazy little child" who seemed to be a burden to everyone. My school life was hell, not just for me but for my parents as well. Not to mention the teachers whom I challenged every day in the classroom. I hated that I was different and at times even hated myself for who I was and what I was doing.

When gathering my research material from the many schools where I was a student, I was embarrassed by a lot of the terrible things I had done. But at the time I did not know what I was doing. I was often confused, not understanding my own actions. I was depressed a lot of the time in my early school days. As I got older it became easier to deal with my problems. I overcame them in a number of ways, including using medication and self-taught techniques that I will discuss in Part Two in greater detail.

Now that I'm nineteen, I look back on my short life, and my childhood seems like a faraway story. I still have no idea why I did things that normal society sees as abnormal. If you or your child has ADD/ADHD, you will understand what I mean when

I say abnormal behavior—those fits of anger and impulsive behavior unleashed on family members that seem to have no reason or specific purpose. It is very hard for parents to deal with and understand why their child is behaving in this abnormal manner. This book, I hope, will help you understand why your child acts in this uncontrolled way.

It was not until I turned nineteen that I seriously considered the challenge of writing this book. After watching a story on children with ADD/ADHD on an Australian current affairs program, I felt that I had to write this book to help other people suffering with what I have endured throughout my life. However, again I put it off. One day it will happen, I thought to myself. I didn't have the time—I had to study at college, and I was going out a lot. But it was really an excuse. I just didn't care enough, I guess. Or maybe it was that I was still embarrassed by my disorder? Most probably a combination of the two.

A young boy down the road from me has ADHD. For the past couple of years my mother has been saying, "Why don't you go talk to the boy's mother?" I usually brushed it aside with "Yeah, maybe later." Then one day I decided to talk to the mother. She was pretty upset with her son's progress at school because he was behind in reading and math. I told her I could not read a short sentence until I was eleven.

It always seems to surprise people when I tell them things about my life at school and home. They often look at me with amazement and even confusion. I believe this is because now I do not act like a *freak,* as my sister called me when I was younger. However, I can understand where this confusion comes from. If you'd said to my parents when I was ten, "Your son will graduate from high school and do well," they would probably have bet their house that this would not happen; if you'd told them their son would go on to college and write a bestselling book, they would have probably bet their lives on that not happening. Well, it did, and this book will tell you about the remarkable turn-around in my life. I hope it will help your child achieve the best results possible.

I have no accredited medical knowledge of ADD/ADHD. However, I do not see how so-called medical experts can really understand ADD/ADHD without actually living with it them-selves. I am not knocking the medical experts, because my doctor is excellent and does understand ADD/ADHD in great depth. But the strategies that I developed myself were invaluable. Instead of ending up in a juvenile detention center, I made it to college.

However, I have skimmed through many books on ADD/ADHD, and they make me very angry because they are often filled with medical mumbo jumbo that really does not help the treatment of your child with ADD/ADHD. They do help partly in understanding what ADD/ADHD is, in a medical sense, which is always a good start for parents. But those books rarely contain techniques and strategies for dealing with ADD/ADHD in daily life. I searched many libraries and on the Internet to find a book by a young person who has ADD/ADHD, and I could not find one. This was a surprise to me. I could not believe that someone had not written a book on their experiences and how they over-came their problems in everyday situations. Well, now someone has, and I guess it's about time!

This book will not give you the answers to all the problems you will come across in managing your child's condition, but it will help. Many parents feel isolated. They feel depressed, confused, and guilty—and of course angry and frustrated. My parents have lost a number of friends throughout my life as a result of my behavior. People would not invite my family to parties and gatherings because I caused too many problems. Along with this, my parents would cut themselves off from people because they were embarrassed by my behavior. My dad told me that they were invited to a lot of parties—but only once! Narrowminded people who did not understand made comments such as, "Leave him with me and I will give him a good belting and pull him in line." My parents were often accused of being bad parents who could not control their son. This was not true, because my sister, Adelaide, who is two years older than me, is the most polite and nicest person you could ever meet. In my younger years my parents took me to see a number of psychiatrists who said it was my parents' fault and that there was nothing wrong with me. How wrong they were!

Now, getting back to the little boy who lives down the street. After offering to help him with his schoolwork, I was quite worried the first time I went to his house. I did not know what to expect. I thought I might have bitten off more than I could chew. Well, the first day I went there his mother showed me his schoolwork: he had to play simple word games that promoted word recognition.

It often took his mother over an hour to get him to do his homework. This hour was mostly taken up with his erratic behavior that included swearing, yelling—basically everything except doing his homework. The first time I went over to their house it took me only fifteen minutes to get him to do his work. I promised to play a Nintendo game with him after he was done.

He had done his work and he knew it, and now he was playing with his Nintendo. His mother told him to get up and do his homework. I told her that he had done it and done it twice. This was accomplished without medication, through techniques I have developed while suffering from this condition. I get great pleasure out of helping people with problems related to ADHD. I enjoy it more because I know how isolated these children feel at school and at home.

I will discuss a number of issues in this book, including picking the right school for your child and selecting the right teacher, if possible. I went to six schools and I know what works and what doesn't. I will talk about other issues, including parenting techniques; anger management; homework, which can be basically impossible for some parents; discipline, what works and what will never work. I know my parents tried everything, including medication, which is always a hot topic in the ADD/ADHD network. I will also discuss relationships among parents and siblings and the child with ADD/ADHD. I hope you will find this book useful in the management of your child. I would just like to add that this book will be most useful only if you are prepared to put in lots of tiring and frustrating hours of work with your child!

I wish you and your child the greatest success in overcoming this challenge, and always remember that the rewards are priceless.

Best wishes,
Benjamin H. Polis

Part One

My Story
(and Helpful Hints
for My Readers)

My First Years: Birth to Age Four

I, Benjamin Heinrich Polis, was born at Sandringham Hospital, Melbourne, Australia, on August 7, 1981. On this day the angels sang out loud, "What have we done?" My life had just started, but my parents' lives changed forever. I was a healthy-looking baby with no obvious physical or mental problems. My parents were pleased that I was normal. It is what all parents hope for in their newborn child. But they were in for a rude shock! My hidden handicap would not be discovered until many years later. Looking back on my early years, my parents have told me there were a number of things in my behavior that appeared to be unusual. Of course I do not remember much, so this information has been recounted by parents and family members.

My mother told me she was not able to breast-feed me in a room with other people in it. Any movement or object in the room distracted me. I stopped feeding and gazed around the room, searching for some other source of entertainment. She overcame this by always removing me to another room. It was the first of many times throughout my life that I was separated or banned from a group. Thinking back, it was probably the first time my parents experienced my short attention span and how easily distracted I was, the classic or common signs of ADD/ADHD. I still have these symptoms and probably will for the rest of my life, but now I understand the problem and I can control my behavior.

I can imagine the first time I started to walk, loving the freedom and thinking, Let's bust out of this place! Well, that's just what I did all the time. For me, no room was a barrier, just another challenge. I always found some ingenious way to bust out and explore this new and exciting world. My mother talks about frequently losing me, searching high and low until she found me, until the next time when she had to start the search again. My father recalls coming home from work to find my mother vacuuming the backyard. I had opened a beanbag and covered the entire yard with white polystyrene balls. Hey, I wanted a white Christmas! (Christmas is in the middle of summer in Australia, so I haven't had one yet.)

Ash Wednesday 1983

Ash Wednesday is the name given to a day in Australian history when bushfires raged across the two southern states of Victoria and South Australia. Many people died and hundreds of houses were destroyed. Every summer during bushfire season in Australia, people think back to that Ash Wednesday.

It was one of the scariest days in my parents' lives. My father remembers looking at the Melbourne horizon and seeing a ring of fire and smoke. It was the first time I was affected by asthma. My parents were in a state of panic because their two-year-old child had begun gasping for breath. Dad rushed me to Frankston Hospital. It was eerie. The streets were deserted since people stayed at home during the bushfires. The air conditioner in the car was sucking in the smoke while I sucked and gasped for life-giving air. I ended up spending a couple of weeks in hospital; it would be the first of many such trips.

The reason I am referring to my experience with asthma is that it taught me we all have our limitations, but we can work around them. And that's exactly what I have done with my ADHD.

Two or three times a year I was rushed to hospital, where I had to stay anywhere from one to three weeks with nurses watching me all the time. My asthma became worse as I got older. When I was about ten, I was rushed from Frankston Hospital to the Royal Children's Hospital in an ambulance, accompanied by a specialist doctor and nurse. I was in intensive care for days with a collapsed lung. My parents were not told at first about the collapsed lung.

I remember one day very clearly. The specialist pulled his chair close to me and said, "If you don't start to look after yourself and take your daily asthma medication, you will be dead in two years." Believe me, from that day on I have taken my asthma medication. I believe the reason that my parents were not told of the severity of my condition was because the doctors were trying to look after not just me but my parents as well. I remember so many incidents when I would call out to my parents in the middle of the night and tell them that I wanted or needed to go to the hospital. I hated going to the hospital but always knew it was the best place for me. Without the excellent care of the staff at both Frankston and the Royal Children's hospitals, I would be dead. So I would like to thank them for all they have done for me and other sick children.

One problem arose time and time again. When I became better I could not sit still, a well-recognized symptom of ADD/ADHD. The doctors said, "Ben should be able to go home in a couple of days." I got so excited and worked myself up so much that I did more harm than good. I ripped the intravenous line out of my vein, jumped out of bed, ran to the cafeteria to buy a Coke and some candy, then ran through the wards and back to my bed. This made me sick again, often worse than before. Then I was told that I could not go home yet. Confused and angry, I cried, staged a whopper of a temper tantrum, threw my pillows and food at the nurses, ripped up my medical charts, and so on.

My parents were upset by my bad behavior but could do nothing to help me. Their little boy wanted to go home but they couldn't take him, because he most probably would die. What a terrible position for my parents, or any parents, to be in! My father often smuggled in a McDonald's burger to cheer me up.

The Children's Hospital was twenty-five miles from home and with the long hours they were working to establish their own real-estate business, it was hard for my parents to see me, but they did. I was scared, confused, and bored sitting in a hospital bed with tubes in my veins and asthma medication pumped into me every ten minutes. I hated being in the hospital. Then one day my father told me, "Grow up. This is the best place for you. You are lucky you don't have diabetes and need insulin shots four times a day." I guess this was the first time I looked at myself in a positive new light. I thought to myself, Hey, you're sick but you're luckier than a lot of other kids. I transferred this positive thought process to how I thought about my ADD/ADHD later in life, especially during my teen years. After I finally accepted that I had ADD/ADHD, and needed to work around it and use it to my advantage, my life became a lot easier.

The first house I grew up in was on a long, busy road. I climbed anything to escape, then ran like the wind down the road, my mother in hot pursuit. If she was watching our front yard too closely, then I ran out the back door, over the fence, into the neighbor's house through their doggie door, and out through their front door—free again!

As I got older and stronger my climbing abilities became greater and I became more daring. I could always climb fences, but now I even climbed over the roof to escape. I could climb anything and would jump from any height. This is characteristic of ADD/ADHD children. They act impulsively, not thinking, even for a brief moment, of the consequences of their actions. Remarkably, I have never broken any bones, but it is interesting to note that ADD/ADHD children are found to have more broken bone injuries than the norm. My advice to parents is to get a good medical plan. You will need it.

My greatest climbing achievement was when I was about three. My mother loved to sew, and she dragged me to every fabric store in Melbourne. Hour after hour she would flick through pattern books and study fabrics while I ran amok. I hated those stores; I still hate them and refuse to go into them, even today. However, I always found a way to amuse myself. I usually climbed over the large rolls and bolts of material. My mother laughs as she tells me that she loved it when I got lost. She deliberately lost me sometimes so she would get some peace and quiet shopping, then she would find me when she was finished.

But one particular day was very different. I climbed on the outside of the escalator all the way to the top, shuffling my feet along a small shelf. The only problem was, I could not get down. This time I do remember telling myself that I was not going to jump. Five meters below me was a hard concrete floor. My mother (still looking at those stupid patterns) was found and she went into a state of panic. From all over the store, people gathered to look at me with fear and amazement, probably thinking, How did that kid get up there? They stopped the escalator and someone brought me down. That was the first and last time I climbed an escalator. But harder and higher structures were soon on the drawing board.

Around age four, my behavior became more destructive and erratic. My grandparents took me to the Royal Melbourne Zoo for a picnic. I ran off to explore. Both grandparents were not worried because I was still in sight and safe. Well, let me rephrase that. I was safe, but the people having nice quiet picnics were not. It was a lovely, sunny day. I had found liquid gold at the end of the rainbow: the main faucet to the extensive watering system for the lawns. With a couple of twists the sprinklers opened up and the entire picnic area was sprayed with water. I ran off, leaving a path of destruction in my wake. It took many minutes before the staff turned off the sprinkler system, but it was too late, everyone's picnic had been flooded. After that, my grandparents hardly ever took me anywhere. I don't know why.

On our long road lived an old, scruffy, brownish red dog. Hour after hour this dog lay across the concrete footpath basking in the hot sun. I hated that dog. Mum and Dad had given me my first bike and I loved it. It gave me freedom and an even faster escape than my little legs. I have fond memories of this bike. I remember every little detail about it. It was bright yellow with a long black seat, in a classic sixties' chopper style. My dad and I had added a couple of minor improvements—noisy plastic beads on the spokes plus a big red flag on a fiberglass pole for my safety. But I believe Dad put this on for other people's safety, not mine—Here I come, get out of my way!

Anyway, back to the dog. I rode all day up and down the footpath in front of our house. On our neighbor's driveway was a ramp made from the curve in the gutter. I rode like a bat out of hell up the road and then made a quick turn onto the ramp to get some airtime. The only problem was that this dog was usually sunbathing on my landing strip. I constantly had to swerve to miss both him and the tree next to him. I crashed many times but always got straight back on my bike and did it all over again.

The dog was my archenemy, but not for long. This day was going to be very different! It was either the dog or me. I made a plan that at the time I thought was foolproof. How wrong I was!

The plan went something like this. I rode all the way to the end of the street, some hundred meters in length. I turned my great yellow bike around and started to ride as fast as my four-year-old legs would let me. I was instantly transformed into that famous motorcycle stunt rider, the great Evel Knievel. The plan was that the dog would be so scared it would quickly move when it saw me coming right for it. Up the ramp I went, faster and higher than ever before. The dog lazily opened one eye and saw me coming, but just lay there, until the great yellow bike and I landed right on him, crushing his ribs. The dog had to be put down, though I suspect some people would say it would have been more fitting for me to be put down.

Thinking and talking about this now is very painful for me. I have no idea why I did it and I am not proud of it. The only explanation I can give is that my impulsiveness once again got the better of me. I could blame it on my ADD/ADHD, but I never have and never will use my ADD/ADHD as an excuse for my actions. Today, I understand that this is the way I am and I can now control my actions. When I was younger, it was nearly impossible. My mother recalls buying flowers for the dog's owner. Over the years, my mother and the flower-shop lady had a very good relationship. My mother said, "I kept her in business." Time after time she bought flowers for people and apologized for the things I had done. It was even more embarrassing for her when she had to give people flowers more than once.

Preschool

At preschool, my parents first experienced the constant embarrassment of having me as their child. Every day my mother picked me up and every day she was bombarded with stories from both the teacher and the parents of the other children. "Ben did this!" and "Ben did that!" Mum hated picking me up; the emotional strain was often too much to handle. This is a regular problem for parents of ADD/ADHD children. They love their child, but it can be so tiring to continually defend him against accusations from others. Sometimes the parents' love turns into frustration, then to anger. Asking—or yelling—at the child "Why did you do that?" will achieve nothing. I did not know my behavior was unacceptable and neither will your child.

I too hated going to preschool because I was always in trouble. I was often confused and suffered from low self-esteem, because I did not know what I was doing wrong. In my mind I was acting normally—my idea of normal, not other people's opinion of normal. I often sat by the entrance, crying uncontrollably while I waited for my mother. I always knew when she was coming to save me because I could smell her distinctive perfume.

The preschool soon got sick of me (like many other schools later in my life) and I pretty much stopped going. When I asked my mother about going to preschool, she laughed and said, "You hardly went there!" I stopped due to an incident with a mentally disabled child. The boy was autistic and tried to strangle people for no reason. Thinking about that now, I guess he did have a reason—we just didn't know what it was. One day this boy strangled and bit me. So I did what any ADD/ADHD child would do: I strangled him back and bit him harder than he had bitten me. I got into so much trouble I refused to go back, and I am sure they were pleased with that. Often a child suffering from ADD/ADHD is labeled bad or uncontrollable and the parents are blamed. All I can say to parents is, keep loving your child. Things will get better as the child grows older and learns to control his behavior and actions.

Family Therapy

Around this time I started seeing child and family psychiatrists. Mum and Dad called them the "family doctors" to nicen it up a bit. I now realize they were embarrassed and trying to hide the fact that their child needed psychiatric help. The whole family went along: Gaye, my mother; Henry, my father; Adelaide, my sister; and me. We all sat around a big room and talked about our problems. I hated talking about our problems because it was always something to do with me. I felt as though they should have just said, "Hey, Ben, you're the problem," and tattooed it on my forehead. The doctors talked to every family member individually, then talked about our problems again, trying to find a solution. We went every Friday to our "family doctor," month after month, year after year.

"What is wrong with him?" my parents asked. The most common answer was: "Nothing, it's just bad parenting techniques; basically you're just bad parents. You'd better come back next Friday so we can talk about this in more detail."

Looking back, I guess it was not the doctors' fault and definitely not my parents'. Our problem was ADD/ADHD, which was not as widely recognized or diagnosed then as it is today. They couldn't help me because they didn't understand the problem. Then there were no support groups or books to help parents understand. It was not until I was twelve that I was diagnosed with attention deficit hyperactivity disorder and received some useful medical help. My parents often felt helpless, not knowing why their son was so upset about everything and everyone. My mother recalls crying herself to sleep on many nights wondering, What can I do? Maybe we are bad parents as the doctors told us. We struggled on as a family, fighting, yelling at each other, and basically just not working as a "normal" family unit.

Family therapy does work; however, it requires a positive effort on the part of everyone involved. Otherwise it can just end up in a slinging match between family members. I believe parents must take a positive role in these meetings. Instead of just talking about all the bad things that happened they must talk up the positive ones. My father was very hotheaded in these meetings and often left the doctor's office screaming. As he walked out, he threw me fifty bucks and told me to get a taxicab home. I was only ten. It is very hard for the ADD/ADHD child, because it seems to him that the whole world is against him. This is how I felt. For this reason I believe parents must make a concerted effort to be positive in family counseling sessions.

The Best Time of My Life: Primary One! Yeah, Right!

For most children, school is a time of great excitement and happiness, but not for me, my parents, or the teachers in the six schools I attended during the next twelve years. I was constantly separated from the class and sent outside. Reading and writing were definitely not my forte. I struggled with every aspect of school life except finding my way to the principal's office. My first school was the nearby state school, and my reputation had preceded me, as it still does today. My mother described how on my first day, one of the teachers greeted us with, "So you're Ben Polis. We've heard all about you. I hope you're not going to cause trouble here." What had they heard about me? Who told them? Was it the preschool teachers? Was it the parents of the preschool children? I don't know, and I would like to say that I don't care. But I do care, because from day one I never had a chance at that school. My mother was furious and hurt.

Unfortunately for me, my behavior attracted the wrong attention. I was dared by the other kids to show my boy's bits to a girl. So I went right up to her and showed her. They thought I was fantastic. (Girls still say that today!) So did I. The girl told the teacher and I was in trouble again. The teacher tried to use reverse psychology on me and asked, "Ben, would you like to show the whole class?" "Okay," I said, and got into trouble again. ADD/ADHD children do not understand situations like these until they are older. What their brains tell them to do isn't always the right thing. It takes a lot of embarrassing experiences and a strong will to overcome this major problem of impulsiveness.

Another incident occurred when the school was assembled in the library to sing and dance to Australian folk songs to celebrate the bicentennial of the landing of Captain Cook. He's the European dude who found Australia. There were maybe fifty to eighty excited children sitting on the floor talking loudly. A teacher walked in and yelled, "Ben Polis! You be quiet!" Instead of telling the whole group to be quiet, I was singled out as the only child making noise. I did not notice this, as I was always singled out for special attention, but it was very noticeable to my mother and all the other parents who had come to see their little darlings participate in the show.

The final straw came a few days later. As part of the celebration, the children had to dress up in period costume.

I went as the famous Australian bushranger, Ned Kelly, who fascinated me at the time. He was an outlaw like Jesse James. He and his gang wore metal armor so the troopers couldn't shoot them. One of my relatives had made an excellent replica of Ned Kelly's armor for me. First, on went the chest armor. Next was a brown, all-weather trench coat, complete with bloody bandages painted with red lipstick to represent the wounds Kelly received when shot by the troopers. Finally, on went the familiar Kelly helmet complete with an eye-slit opening; and I had a pistol in each hand. I really looked the part. My father delivered me to school and observed what happened. I was late and everyone was already in class. When I walked into the room the class erupted, clapping and cheering. They knew it was me because I'd been the only one missing from the class roll call. The teacher barely moved, just looked up from his desk, told the class to be quiet, and told me to take off my ridiculous costume, put it at the back of the room, and sit down at my desk. What a letdown! I was admired by the class but put down again by another teacher.

My father was watching this through the glass windows in the corridor. Furious, he stormed out of the school and told my mother what had happened. To my parents it was obvious I had been labeled by the teachers. I was not going to get a fair go. I was about to leave my first school after only six months.

I don't really care anymore. What's done is done, I guess. But in those days I hated school. I was not stupid; I just couldn't concentrate like other kids, which affected my behavior and my learning ability. I would go to school crying, cry at school, and then come home crying. It was not that I was a crybaby and liked crying. It was, I guess, that I never knew exactly why I was in trouble. To the teachers, I was a bad kid who disrupted the class too often. Schools are not made for children like me. But schools can and should recognize the problems of an ADD/ADHD child and all children. Passing problem students such as me from school to school resolves nothing. It only causes more problems for such students. They often leave school as soon as they can without completing their studies. This makes me sad because if I had left school prematurely, as many ADD/ADHD children do, I would not have the academic grounding I do today—and this book would not have been written.

It makes me laugh to look back at my report cards now. Nothing really changed from primary one to sixth year. They all go like this:

> Benjamin has the ability to do better but needs to focus more of his extensive energy into doing more useful and productive things. He lacks good concentration skills and has trouble listening to instructions. He often involves himself in inappropriate activity such as entertaining the class by being the center of attention.

In my early school days, my language and mathematics skills were often cause for concern. My sports abilities were always excellent and this was something I enjoyed. Sports are a great way for children with ADD/ADHD to burn off excess energy. I still use exercise as a tool to help me settle down. Sports also give these children a chance to build self-esteem, which is often hard to achieve in the classroom. Lack of self-esteem was a problem that I had to overcome in my early years. This age is crucial for children. It is when they learn essential interpersonal skills, when they learn to love or hate school. Well, my feelings toward school developed pretty quickly. I hated it!

In the classroom, impulsiveness and standing out are a bad mixture. The problem arises due to low self-esteem. ADD/ADHD children often fall behind in their schoolwork, receive the unwanted attention of the teacher, become separated from other children, and suffer from low self-esteem. The ADD/ADHD child is constantly being made to feel different from the rest of the kids. The ADD/ADHD child wants to be "normal" but does not understand why he or she is not. They look the same but just don't seem to fit in with the rest of the children. Other children often use an ADD child as a scapegoat. When the ADD/ADHD child is told to do something by the other kids, he or she goes at it like a bull at a gate. This is caused by impulsiveness—not thinking before acting. It is often harder for ADD/ADHD kids to say no than yes. As a parent, you must try to build self-esteem in your child.

My problem was that I loved being the center of attention and still do. I usually did the most foolish things just to get a laugh. This is why I was in so much trouble when I was young. Now I understand and realize that the other kids were just using me as a bit of a joke.

    I spent most of my early school days sitting in the punishment corner wondering what was wrong with me. My parents remember me dressed in my school uniform crying, every day pleading with them to let me stay home. Something had to change and it did. They reasoned that maybe a private school with smaller classes would help. Well, off to a private school I went, tie and all!

Private School: Primary One to Four

The private school was expensive and had smaller classes, but for me nothing changed, except that the teachers could spend more time with individual students.

The report card on page 20 looks good, but in my opinion it's not accurate. I couldn't do the work that most of the children could. I could not read, spell, or write and I did not enjoy books. I was far below standard in all areas except sports. I could not read the most basic words or complete basic math. The conclusion I have drawn from this is that the new school was not going to tell my parents that I was academically not up to standard, compared to the other students, especially when they were paying thousands of dollars a year.

PRIMARY ONE REPORT CARD

Expression	Grade	
Listening skills	B	Ben's oral expression is clear and confident and his
Oral expression	B	written expression has shown great improvement.
Written expression	C	Ben generally makes an effort to listen attentively.

Reading	Grade	
Oral reading	C	Ben tries hard in reading and is developing quite
Comprehension	B	well. He enjoys books and makes good use of the
Word attack skills	C	class and school library.

Spelling	Grade	
Spells assigned words	B	Ben has worked very hard to develop his spelling
Applies spelling skills in writing	B	skills with very good results, both in written work
		and with set words.

Handwriting	Grade	
Letter formation	B	Ben's handwriting is quite fluent with good letter
Fluency	B	formation when he takes the time to write carefully.
Book work/Organization		(Not Shown)

Physical Education	Grade	
Motor skills	A	Ben is very aggressive toward his sport. He is a coordinated and confident student.
Participation	B	Ben is still learning tolerance toward those who do not perform as well as he does. He is making progress in this regard.

Social Behavior and Learning Skills

Respects the rights of others	Not seen yet
Accepts constructive criticism	Excellent
Participates actively	Excellent
Courteous in speech and manner	Not seen yet
Relates well	Not seen yet
Begins work promptly	Not seen yet
Concentrates on tasks	Excellent
Shares duties willingly	Excellent
Helps others in need	Not seen yet
Organizes own belongings	Not seen yet

Primary Two

At this time I continued to struggle with both schoolwork and behavior. My reading and writing were getting better, but my skills were still below average. My teacher at the time was Mrs. Yates. I would like to say thank you to this lovely person who had the patience and cared enough to help me to learn how to read. Without her, this would not have been possible. It was Mrs. Yates who recognized my reading and spelling problems and instigated a reading-recovery program. She said to me that if I was willing, she would spend an hour with me every day after school to work on my English. I said yes and my parents said yes, too, because they scored a free babysitter! So every day after school I stayed with her and learned the basics of reading. During this period I truly thought I was just *stupid*! I remember one occasion as if it were yesterday. She asked me to spell "of," and I sounded out the word and spelled it "ov"—the way it sounds. It was obviously wrong and I couldn't believe how dumb I was. I could not even spell a basic two-letter word correctly. It's words like this that make learning English so hard and frustrating. It's difficult trying to explain to a child that he must remember and then learn how to use words, but that not all words can be simply sounded out. This is especially difficult when teaching an ADD/ADHD child. Short-term memory problems are common with ADD/ADHD students and magnify the difficulty in remembering some words, such as "of," commonly found in English.

Mrs. Yates and I persisted every day after school, and I continued studying with my parents at home. I hated reading and still hate forced reading today, such as massive college books. The problem is not with the reading itself or the content of the book.

Children with ADD/ADHD don't have the concentration and patience to continue reading when it gets boring for them so quickly. To tell the truth, I read my first book from cover to cover only a couple of months ago. Maybe you find that hard to believe, but it is true. I think it is quite amusing and some people may think it is impossible that a nineteen-year-old college student who finished reading his first book only a couple of months ago is now writing his own.

While reading my first book ever, I wondered how I could keep interested and concentrate on one topic for hours on end. I thought about this a lot, and then it hit me—I wasn't reading the book as I used to. I was part of the book. Instead of reading words, I was visualizing what the words were saying. This was a real breakthrough for me and I will describe in Part Two how you can use this technique with your own child's education. It really works wonders. I hated reading anything at school. I didn't even read my three novels in sixth year English, and that was my second best subject overall. My mother went to extraordinary lengths to help me read my sixth year English novels. She rang up the Blind Society and got them on tape for me. I didn't use the tapes, but I did lend them to my friends at school and they found them very useful. When they gave them back to me, I lost some of the tapes. The Blind Society called to get them back, and I didn't have the courage to tell them that I had lost them. So I used my quick-thinking ADD/ADHD brain and told the lady, "I am blind and I can't see them or find them!" She had pity on me and I felt so bad! But Mum sent them a check because she felt bad, too!

To overcome this problem, find out what your child is interested in and use it to your advantage. My parents did this by using

Teenage Mutant Ninja Turtles trading cards (a fad with children at the time). I was obsessed with these cards. The cards had only a little bit of information on the back. I was able to focus enough to read them every night because they interested me. This is where you can put your child's obsessions to good use.

As my academic skills improved, my confidence increased. Once your child has mastered the basic words, he or she should progress at an impressive speed. This is because he is not stupid; he just learns differently. In the later chapters I will discuss techniques that show you how to tap into your child's interests and capture that elusive attention span. This may seem strange but I can study for twelve hours straight (without medication) using the self-help techniques I have developed.

This is the comment from my primary two teacher, Mrs. Yates:

> Ben is a pleasant, reliable member of the class. He is always ready to help someone in trouble. The improvement he is making in reading and spelling is giving him a great boost in confidence, which is very good to see. I hope this continues in the second half of the year.

With a lot of hard work my academic progress improved greatly. But my behavior was still an issue. One day our class went outside to play a game, I don't remember exactly what it was. A girl was doing handstands in the sports shed while we were waiting for the teacher. I joined in and also did a handstand. She pushed me over and I fell. Well, I was so angry at her that when she did another handstand I pushed her over with extreme force.

This is a common reaction of ADD/ADHD children. They don't think about the consequences of their actions. They just act. She fell over and started crying. I was sent to the principal's office without any explanation and without being able to give my side of the story. Situations like this happened often. The ADD/ADHD child is always the one who gets in trouble when in his own mind he has done nothing wrong. This creates a lot of confusion and greatly upsets him because he does not understand why he is always getting into trouble. I was outside the principal's office, waiting to be blasted again. I thought to myself, Well, I'm not wanted here, so I took off and ran away from school.

The school was on a long road with farms on both sides. I ran up the road with the school principal in hot pursuit in the school bus. It would have looked pretty amusing for anyone driving past. I was caught, taken back to school, and got into even more trouble. I hated school so much! I had to go back but word had spread about my daring activities. Even the older kids were impressed. From that day on I was known as the kid who had run away from school.

Primary Three

Nothing much changed in primary three except that I had a new teacher who could not handle me and I couldn't handle her. She hated me and I hated her. We had a personality conflict. She was a strong feminist, who didn't like hyperactive, rude, and opinionated students like me. She was straight out of teachers' college and not ready for a boy like me. She highlighted my mistakes to the class, always pointing her finger at me. The girls in the class were her favorites and they knew it. They blamed me for everything that went wrong in class. These girls and I have spoken about her since, and they still laugh when they tell me how they got away with everything by using me as the scapegoat. As a consequence of my ill treatment, my anger and behavior problems at home escalated. The more I got into trouble at school the more confused I became, and this then came out in my home life. I constantly hit my sister, the dog, anybody and anything, just to release my anger. I was out of control. I knew it and my parents knew it. I know that I was out of control because I contemplated suicide because I hated myself so much and I didn't know why. People often ask me about suicide when I do public speaking and it makes me very uncomfortable, because now I wouldn't even dream of it. But I say to them that very young children do think about it. And their response is that kids don't understand what it means. This is true. However, some kids do think they have no other option. When you are in your teens, you can run away or just leave school. It's something that people seem to forget about in children younger than ten. They do have the same thoughts as adults and teens. They are just very naïve and immature.

Primary Four

Well, I got the same teacher again for primary four. I feel this should not be allowed. It is extremely unfair for children who do not like a teacher, because their studies will be affected. I fell further and further behind in class and my parents became extremely worried. It was during this time the principal recommended I see another child psychiatrist. This is the report written by the psychiatrist to my parents.

Confidential Psychological Report
Name: Ben Polis
Referred By: Principal of College

Ben presented as an energetic eight-year-old child who attends local private college. He has a ten-year-old sister (Adelaide) who attends a primary school. Mr. Polis was concerned at Ben's behavior and seemed extremely willing to gain help for himself and family as well as for Ben, to understand and learn how to control Ben's behavior.

Mr. Polis told me that Adelaide was very socially accepted and usually exhibited excellent behavior, but Ben, although happy, was causing problems at home and, to a lesser extent, at school because of his behavior. Ben suffers from asthma and has previously seen a child psychiatrist.

I saw Ben on four occasions and spoke with Mr. Polis on each of these. I spoke with Adelaide on one occasion. Mrs. Polis did not attend any sessions. It is my opinion that Ben's behavior signifies an attention deficit disorder with hyperactivity. Ben's behaviors include inattentiveness, impulsivity, aggression, and disobedience.

When dealing with a child who exhibits this type of behavior, parents need to be aware of the following: While a "normal" child might not want to do something, the hyperactive child will refuse point-blank and have a tantrum if pressed. The child has trouble remembering instructions; a firm *"no"* is forgotten within hours.

Because his brain becomes intensely overstimulated by any mental exertion, instructions of any kind tend to evoke a wild and uncontrolled response. Be prepared to repeat many,

many more times all the edicts and instructions the "normal" child learns and remembers quite quickly.

Most hyperactive children do not respond to voice alone. This is not deliberately ignoring the parent, but because they do not process incoming information in the normal way. Even the sound of their own name, repeated several times, may not get a response. Try touching the child to attract attention.

Get him to look at you and focus his attention on you before you speak. Shouting at him will produce more confusion in his brain and may make him have a tantrum. If this child's confidence in his parents is undermined by mixed messages it magnifies the problem, therefore it is extremely important that he receive consistent messages from both parents about behavior and how they feel about him as a person.

There is growing evidence that allergies can cause hyperactivity in a susceptible child. The children may be allergically sensitive to foods and also sensitive to inhaled allergens. Ben and his family need to be aware, because of his asthma and hyperactivity, of his food intake (diet) and inhalants. Ben needs to be disciplined in this area. He needs a lot of positive reinforcement when he is behaving well and often needs things explained more than other children need to have. His food intake needs to be monitored to see what foods cause his behavior to increase or stabilize.

If there are any further issues you would like to discuss with me, I will be happy to do so.

Searching through my extensive medical records and finding this report was a surprise to my parents because we thought I had been finally diagnosed when I was twelve years old, but it clearly states that I was diagnosed when I was eight. The problem was that ADD/ADHD was not readily recognized and treated then as it is today. This has changed substantially with ADD/ADHD becoming better recognized worldwide. The psychiatrist recommended better parenting techniques and modifying my diet. Unfortunately this was not the solution.

Due to my allergic reactions to foods that caused asthma, my diet had always been regulated. My parents fed me only healthy foods that were not pumped full of chemicals. Because if they did, my asthma flared up.

I was never placed on a specific controlled diet for my ADD/ADHD. I used to believe that diet did not have a lot to do with ADD/ADHD; however, my opinion has changed in recent years.

I didn't believe that diet could greatly change the psychological makeup of one's brain, and studies state that only 5 percent of subjects show any improvement when their diets are modified.

However, social change has played a major role in my opinion changing. Obesity is a global problem, especially in children. For this reason, and this reason alone, I now believe that diet has got a lot more to do with ADD/ADHD. Not directly in a psychological sense but in an overall health and well-being sense. I have no doubt that modified diets could reduce hyperactivity because we have all seen what happens when kids drink too many fizzy drinks. So basically what I am saying is that a healthy diet can't hurt and would have to help, as it has been proven to improve learning retention and the overall well-being of a child.

My parents were good parents and strictly controlled my behavior. We found out later I simply needed medication to increase my concentration and learning retention. Before we go on, let me please state firmly that I do not believe that medication by itself is the solution to modifying a child's ADD/ADHD behavior. Medication is not the answer to ADD/ADHD and never will be! Your child must learn to control his behavior, learn to adjust and modify the way he acts. And parents who love their child must help and show him how. I could concentrate when I had to. I could do the work when I had to, and I could behave well when I wanted to. But I didn't then, because I simply did not know how to turn on my concentration and modify my behavior, as I do now.

Hints for the First School Years

The first years of schooling are very important—not only academically but socially. If your child has bad experiences with teachers or fellow students, these experiences may affect him in later years. If he develops a hatred for a teacher or a subject, he may retain this negative attitude his whole school life.

My tip in the early years is to try above all else to keep your child happy. Academic ability is not the most important thing. It was during these early years that I really started to hate school. I remember crying and begging my parents to let me stay home. I hated the way I felt while at school. I was treated differently by my teachers and peers because I was different. I knew I was different at a very early age, and this is especially hard because it is during these early years that children develop their sense of self.

Help your child be healthy and happy by putting less emphasis on making grades and more on making friends. Try to get your child involved in activities with his peers. This should be a fun time in a child's life.

Academically, I was pretty unsuccessful in my early school career. This problem often arises with ADD/ADHD children. They are not stupid, are often quite bright. But they learn in totally different ways from other children. The only problem is that ADD/ADHD children usually must learn in the conventional manner. To overcome this, many parents employ remedial tutors or do a lot of one-on-one teaching with their child. Primary one through four is a difficult period for both the parents and the child. The child must learn to read and write or face falling behind in school and subsequently in life.

Here are the major problems. The child does not have the same attention span as other children and loses interest very quickly. Homework is often an issue that ends in tears, yelling, and sometimes violent conflict. The child falls further and further behind until he is so far behind the other children that he believes he is truly stupid. The ADD/ADHD child is often seen as a daydreamer in class. This is because other more exciting thoughts are going on inside his head.

Unfortunately, there is no easy answer. As a parent, you must persist until your child can read and write at a level that will allow him to progress to higher classes. ADD/ADHD children often repeat grades in their early years. I strongly disagree with this policy because it contributes to a major problem—low self-esteem. The ADD/ADHD child already feels different, isolated, and stupid. Leaving him behind just reinforces this belief.

I am currently tutoring a boy who told me, "The other kids don't have to do this extra work."

I replied, "You're right, the kids don't have to do this work because they have already done it a couple of years ago." We had a little talk about this. I tried to explain to him that everyone has to learn to read and that it takes time. I told him that he had been wasting his time by mucking around and not doing his homework. I asked him, "Do you want to read?"

He replied, "Yes."

"What's stopping you then?"

He replied, "Nothing, I guess."

"That's not true. You are stopping yourself. Why?"

His answer, "I don't know."

I then asked him again, "Do you want to read?"

Again he replied, "Yes, I told you that."

Making him think to himself, Why can't I read like the other kids? made crucial progress in this situation. Once he realized that he himself was the reason he could not read, his effort increased dramatically and so did his results.

When using this technique of trying to make your child accept responsibility for his lack of progress in something, you must pick your words very carefully. You must make sure not to further damage the child's already low self-esteem. You must make the child feel that he can do anything that he puts his mind to. Once he achieves something he had thought he could not do, you can use this achievement to reinforce a positive thought process.

This technique comes from my own personal experiences. My father always told me, "You can do it!" At the age of five I could ski better than most adults. My father taught me by holding me between his legs and then letting me go so I had to ski by myself. If I crashed and started crying, my father said "Get up!" Then we did it all over again. Every time I fell I got up and did it all again. I became so good my father took me down the hardest runs, mostly on my backside. When we got to the bottom he told me that I had just completed a black run (the hardest run).

The next time he told me we were going down a black run and I didn't want to go, he said, "You have done it before. Did you get hurt?" I replied, "No." "So what's stopping you? Let's go!"

When I realized I could do anything, my confidence sky-rocketed. I became so good, I skied around adults who had fallen, sprayed snow all over them, and yelled out "Suffer!" This occurred many times, and my father punished me because during the long wait for the next chairlift, he saw adults glaring at him. But I still kept on doing it. It was too much fun!

You must find something, anything that your child is good at, to build self-esteem. Sports are extremely useful for all children at this age, but especially for ADD/ADHD children. When competing in sports, their unlimited supply of energy and eagerness often shines brightly. I believe individual sports are best for young ADD/ADHD children, who are often isolated in team sports due to their behavior. Individual sports create excellent self-esteem because the kids find they did it all by themselves. It also allows these children an outlet to let off steam, instead of releasing their anger and frustration on their parents. ADD/ADHD children often get bored doing the same thing, so when this happens you need to be prepared to change to or try another sport. Most important, try to get your child to pick the next sport. This makes him responsible for his actions and avoids the problem when he says, "It's your fault, Mum. You made me do this!" This idea of encouragement and trying to create a positive mental attitude is not a new concept, but it is a crucial tactic for any parent trying to overcome low self-esteem in a child, particularly in the early school years.

I guess what I am asking is: How do parents and teachers expect to control a child who can't control his own behavior? It is impossible . . . unless you teach the child to understand his own behavior, which will be discussed later.

Major Family Disasters

Little Boys Shouldn't Play with Big Boys' Toys

It was Easter 1990 and five families went to Cape Paterson, a Victorian seaside vacation resort town, to surf, fish, and just relax. Not this year though, for Benjamin Polis had arrived. We stayed in the local trailer park facing the roaring ocean of Bass Strait. My father and his friend were keen skin divers, snorkeling for fish with a speargun or a Hawaiian sling, a spear about two meters long with barbed points at one end and a strong elastic rubber band at the other end which fires the spear at the fish. I was only nine years old but, boy, do I remember this vacation. One day my father and his mate came back from skin diving and left their spears at the front of the caravan. I grabbed my dad's Hawaiian sling to show my cousin Lachlan how it worked, shooting it vertically about ten meters into the air. I repeated this a number of times, until a strong gust of wind blew the spear onto the power lines. It created a short circuit between the two wires. This all happened in the blink of an eye. The power pole that Lachlan and I were standing under exploded with sparks flying everywhere. It looked like a bad day in Bosnia. The current then flowed through all the other poles, blowing them up one after another in a big circle around the caravan park. Every power line connected between the poles fell to the ground, just missing tents and vans. People came running to see what had happened. I don't know how it was that no one was killed or injured. The only wires that did not fall were the two with the aluminum spear still lying across them. A state electricity commission team arrived to repair the damage.

I did not see any of this because I hid in our camper for hours in my bunk, covered with sleeping bags. Frightened, like any other child I thought that what I could not see could not hurt me. I remember thinking to myself, I can't do anything right. Even now, thinking back, this was a period in my life that still makes me upset. I wanted to die and even contemplated killing myself. This seems pretty sad when you remember that I was only nine, but I lived through this nightmare over and over when I was younger. I was different, stupid, always in trouble, and everyone hated me. Well, that's not true, but that's what I thought at the time.

Dad told me that after the repair team worked most of the day on the lines, the foreman asked some people, including Dad, about the incident. The foreman asked, "Do you know who did this? Now, before you answer, I am telling you the repair bill for the damage is around thirteen thousand dollars, and if the parents of the boy who did this had any sense, they would pack up immediately and leave the park. Do you know what I mean?" My father may be honest, but he is not stupid. And that's what we did, and we have never gone back to Cape Paterson since. I would just like to thank the man who told my dad that we had to leave because otherwise I would still be paying the bill today.

The above is an example of an ADD/ADHD child doing something without realizing the consequences of his actions. I could not foresee that playing with a spear near power lines could result in so much damage and possibly kill someone. My parents were upset, but I was not punished in any way. It was bad enough that I was punishing myself. I could understand being punished by my parents, but what would that have achieved? More important was my mental condition. Feeling stupid, always getting into trouble, I needed support, not more punishment. Fortunately, I got support from my parents and that is my advice to other parents. Don't punish a child who is already down. No matter how hard it is at times, you must support your child, particularly at the worst of times. If you punish him and give no support when he is fragile and vulnerable, who will support him when he needs it the most?

Let's now consider another situation where two ADD/ADHD symptoms combine—impulsiveness with determination/stubbornness. I wrote the following story in sixth year for an English assignment. It was meant to be a creative writing exercise, but the story is true, like everything else in this book.

He Who Dares Wins!

As I look back on my childhood there is one significant experience I remember. It is still as vivid as the night it all unfolded. It was around four o'clock in the afternoon when my family and I set off from our campsite that was on land adjacent to a national park. The national park was about thirty

miles from the heart of Sydney. As we set off on the walking
trail it seemed to be engulfed by a veranda of vines and scrub
that encircled us as we walked farther and farther into the
unknown. It seems somewhat foolish now looking back on it,
but we were more interested in our conversation than where
we were walking.

As the day passed and dusk set in, the night sky darkened
with every step and the conversation intensified. I began to
question my parents about what might be lurking in the thick
scrub. The scrub was now only a vision of dark shadows that
seemed to join with the night sky. "Scared, Ben?" Dad asked.
I replied, "No." But I was only ten and I truly was scared of
the dark and especially the uncertainty of the moment. My
parents and my older sister, Adelaide, began to tease and
taunt me about the fictional boogeyman that I believed in. I
was continually being asked, "Is that the boogeyman, Ben?
Oooooo!" I fell behind, and they let me continue alone along
the path. My mother then dared me to walk back to the caravan by myself, for one hundred dollars. This was a lot of
money at the time for a ten-year-old. After a couple of minutes of weighing the pros and cons, the fact that I was a mad
Ninja Turtles fan at the time swayed my decision. Thinking
of how many new figurines I could buy with the money, I set
off by myself back to the campsite to win and claim my prize.

I thought that the quickest and most accurate way to get
home was to walk straight ahead and follow the lights twinkling
on the horizon like the stars in the sky. Walking soon developed
into a fast jog, trying not to think of the boogeyman that every
few seconds flashed through my mind like a recurring nightmare. Running, I focused my entire attention straight ahead on
the Ninja Turtles that I could buy, if only I made it!

Meanwhile, my parents thought that I would turn around and find them. They planned that when I did they would all jump out and scare the hell out of me. They did not believe that I would walk home alone. After realizing that I was not coming after them, they ran around frantically searching. By this time I had made it and started to wonder where my family was. To kill time, I took some money from my mum's handbag. I intended to pay it back with my one hundred dollars, which I was beginning to long for. I set off to play video games in the games room in the camping park.

My parents by this stage had got themselves lost and finally made their way to a ranger's house in the national park. Well, the ranger got on the phone to his mates and within fifteen minutes they had six rangers searching and scouring the bush, now totally immersed by the cover of darkness. A couple of hours later, sitting in my tent because the games room had closed, I started to panic. "Where is my family?" Many hours later they turned up to find me in my bunk fast asleep.

This experience shows my early determination to succeed when pushed hard enough by myself. This is something that I must do every day because I can be very lazy when I do not force myself. For example, writing this book. Like a lot of things, it frustrates me and I give up easily when things get too hard or boring. However, I force myself to do things by shutting myself off from everyone. Sometimes I feel a bit like the Dalai Lama, putting myself in self-imposed exile by shutting myself off from the outside world. I have such trouble concentrating that when I do finally start something I must not let things distract me, such as the television or a phone call.

Primary Five and Off to Another School

It was the first day of primary five at the private school with a new teacher. He was a good teacher and all the children loved him. He was a tough but fair man—just what I needed. My parents and I thought it was good for me to have a male teacher who would be able to handle my boisterous behavior, especially since I had usually had female teachers.

Things were looking good for me. However, my hatred of my previous teacher still burned like a wildfire, so I did something incredibly stupid. I wanted to pay her back for the way she had treated me for the past two years. Someone had passed around a picture of two people having sex. I just happened to have brought it to school! So I thought, Right, I'll get her this time! First, I wrote the name of her boyfriend on the man's head. He was on top of the woman in a very promiscuous pose. Then I wrote her name on the woman's head. I put a talking bubble coming from my ex-teacher's mouth with the words, "Ooo, baby!" and then stuck it in the teacher's diary so that when she opened it up the following day she would have a pleasant surprise. Well, I guess she did because I got expelled the next day!

That was a rude shock to me because I never thought I would be expelled from school. Well, I was wrong and it was the first of many schools that would use the big E word on me. My parents were not pleased when I was kicked out. However, it did improve their cash flow. Dad called the nearest state school and told them they had a new student. There was some objection because the school was already full. But by this stage, I think my father had had enough. He told the principal that the law required his son to be educated; this was the nearest state school and this was where his son would be going.

My new school was good, and I had a teacher who could really handle me. He made me hate him because he was just like me and challenged me in every way. I was always trying to show him up by being a big shot and the class clown. I have always had a problem with authority and still do. I don't care who someone is or what position he holds. I treat people who deserve to be respected with respect, but if I feel they do not deserve respect from me, they get none. This would get me into trouble at school and at work when I was older. This teacher was always throwing me out of class when I cracked a joke or was just being myself, which was being a typical ADD/ADHD kid. The problem was in my mind. He did not practice what he preached. If he could crack jokes all the time, why couldn't I? He was the teacher and I was the student, but I couldn't see the difference because of my lack of respect for authority. I don't know why I had this attitude toward my superiors. I guess it was because I was always in trouble. It was always me against them or something. . . .

During primary five I spent many weeks in the Children's Hospital again with asthma. I still have many get-well cards from students and teachers, and it makes me laugh when I read them. The card my primary five classmates gave me is so true and pretty funny. The card goes something like this:

GET WELL SOON

To Dear Ben,

    It gets a bit quiet in the classroom when you're not here and I've got no one to pick on. So get well quick and get back here!

                          From your teacher

The Students' Comments

To Ben, it's not funny at school anymore!
Get back here, it's boring without cha!
To Ben, you don't annoy us anymore!
To Ben, I hope you get well soon.
P.S. I hope you come back so I can see you get into trouble!

In primary five my academic work improved substantially. I believe that the new school was good for me because the children came from average families. This made it easier to interact with them. The kids played sports at lunchtime and were a lot more boisterous. This was great for me or any ADD/ADHD child who has excess energy to burn. I took up Australian Rules football, which gave me another avenue to release my anger and frustration rather than directing it at my parents and teachers. My school report had the following comments:

English: A great improvement in attitude toward language work in general has allowed Ben to achieve a lot this year.

Mathematics: Has the potential to do well when he puts his mind to it. Ben displays the skills necessary to produce results.

General Studies: A big effort is needed to be a cooperative member of a group. Occasionally he shows he possesses excellent knowledge and skills.

Art: Ben has good artistic skills but tends not to display them due to a lack of concentration.

General Comments: Ben has shown great improvement in his attitude toward his work. With a greater effort to stay on task and not enter into every conversation in the classroom without thinking about the consequences of his actions, his work will improve even more. Ben also needs to show a little more compassion toward the other children and not attempt to talk over them all the time.

Primary Six

During primary six my behavior became worse, and I was constantly assaulting students, my parents, and my sister. I was always bigger than the other kids because I developed earlier. I believe I was violent and always hitting out because I hated who I was. This anger and hatred was then focused on the rest of the world.

Homework was always a problem, and this was a serious concern for my parents because I was just about to enter middle school. I had joined a basketball team and I assaulted one of my teammates because he was annoying me. Incidents like this were regular during the year. Neither my parents nor teachers could control me anymore. I was growing up and fast. I did what I wanted, when I wanted.

This school, like all my schools, had finally had enough of me, especially my art teacher. Children with ADD/ADHD can do well if they have artistic flair. Art has never been one of my strong points. Like a lot of ADD/ADHD children, the problem I have is that any unstructured classroom setup is often too overwhelming. Doing woodwork, textiles, and art often needs a high level of concentration. To try to get an ADD/ADHD child to paint a picture on his own is nearly impossible. An ADD/ADHD child is often distracted by all the paints and tools. Eating the paint or painting the kid next to him can be more appealing than focusing on the task in front of him. This is not the case in all situations. An ADD/ADHD child can do well if he really enjoys the subject.

However, I did not enjoy them. Well, that's not true: I did enjoy the subjects because they were so much fun—I could get up to so much mischief. On an academic scale I did not do well. An example of this was fifth year woodwork. I chose this subject because it was a breeze. Well, I thought it would be a breeze. Anyway, I nearly failed woodwork in fifth year. It was not that I couldn't do the work, it was that I was more interested in talking and just having fun.

Also, these subjects are usually at the end of the day in a double period. By the end of the day an ADD/ADHD child can hardly concentrate enough to tie his shoelaces. This is a huge problem. You place an ADD/ADHD child in a class like this at the end of the day, when his concentration is at its lowest point, and expect him to work independently in a classroom full of distraction? It ain't going to happen! This is a recipe for disaster.

This was just as true for me in primary six. Visualize the following situation. It was the last twenty minutes on a Friday after a long week and I was not at my best. I was tired, frustrated, and bored. I had to make something out of clay fast. I had been fooling around rolling out a two-foot penis. I then had a brainwave: "Let's make a face that looks like a penis." Very amusing for an

ADD/ADHD child and the other students. I cleverly molded the clay into shape. The penis at first looked like a nose, but then was readily recognizable as a penis, with eyes that looked like testicles and added hair which resembled pubic hair. I finished my masterpiece in the nick of time. I placed my artwork on the teacher's desk so she could put it in the kiln. Did she like my masterpiece? No, she nearly died! The following Monday my father and I were summoned to see the principal and the art teacher. I remember this so clearly, I thought it was the funniest thing ever! My art teacher said calmly and politely, "Benjamin made a very large male anatomy!" I denied it for about ten minutes. "It's a face! I don't see what's wrong with it. I like it!" Anyway, they wanted to expel me, but again my dad pleaded with them to let me stay.

My parents and teachers soon observed a pattern in my behavior. I was constantly in trouble, usually in the afternoon, because I was tired and bored. This pattern continued into my high school years. What I am trying to say is that if you can prevent your ADD/ADHD child from having those types of classes in the afternoon it will be beneficial for both you and the school. Unfortunately in primary school you have little control over schedules. In high school you can choose your subjects to a certain degree. You need to be prepared for trouble in afternoon classes and explain to the school why it happens. It is also worth noting that stimulant medication often wears off in the afternoon, only adding to the problem.

Every day I furiously rode my bike out of the school and did a big burnout in front of all the parents waiting to pick up their children. Many parents hated me and gave me glares and stares. I loved this and deliberately picked on their children. It was a big game for me and I loved the attention. The common belief was that I acted in such a manner because I was a spoiled brat, because my parents were well-off. This impression followed me everywhere I went. I always had the newest brand-name shoes and clothes and rubbed it in to others. I am so competitive in everything I do and I hate to lose. This may be due to the low self-esteem I had when I was younger. Other children would be my friends until they came to our house and saw that I had lots of toys and so on. Then they ignored me at school.

This also happened at sports clubs. When I was eleven I joined the local cricket club, and my dad bought me all the new gear as soon as I started. The other kids were so jealous, they picked on me and pushed me around. One Saturday I ran off from the cricket ground where we were playing. I walked home, and it took me hours. Schools and sports clubs—I changed them often because I wore out my welcome. Eventually, this was resolved by taking me out of our area to play cricket in a wealthier suburb. I still can't understand why people reacted this way—it was not my fault my parents could afford to buy things.

You may be thinking that I deserved this treatment because I boasted about having all these great things. But this did not happen until I was much older. I turned it into a game. If people were going to be jealous of me because I had new clothes all the time, I could not do anything about it. I was not going to take back the new clothes my parents had bought me, was I? So instead I turned it around and sought enjoyment by deliberately showing off my new things. They were going to dislike me anyway so I just made them hate me even more.

Because of my bad behavior everyone in the area knew me, for the wrong reasons. A real-estate agent must cultivate a good reputation to get work in his area. I was such a monster my parents believed people would not want to use my father as their agent. They thought I was bad for their business. To overcome my bad name in the area (after three schools and three sports clubs), I started going to schools farther and farther away. My parents always joked I would end up in Darwin, which is three thousand miles away, because I had worn out my welcome in our home state of Victoria. They also discussed sending me to a boarding school in Darwin because I would not be able to run home as I could and did in Melbourne. They were only joking—I think. . . .

School Hints Up Through Primary Six

Start building independence around primary five and definitely by primary six. It is a massive shock to the system for most kids when they start middle school. But for an ADD/ADHD child it can be disastrous. Therefore prepare yourself by helping your child become independent. Start making your son accountable for his actions. Stop babying him, because once he goes to middle school it is a whole different ball game.

During these years, you should start to promote self-education. If you are able to get your son into a good homework routine, he can take this into high school. If your son struggles academically— as many ADD/ADHD children do—this must be addressed before he gets to high school. Yes, this is a very hard task, but if it is not addressed he may have the shock of his life when he gets to high school. High school is usually a bigger place and therefore there is a greater chance that your son will fall through the cracks of the education system. Try to establish a good relationship with your son in regards to schoolwork, and be a part of his life.

I also think it's a good time to start having the-birds-and-the-bees talk with your son. Kids go through puberty at different ages. It can be a frightening experience when things start happening to your body and you don't fully understand what's going on.

My Diagnosis of ADHD

During first year my behavior became so bad my mother could not handle me anymore. She was determined to find out what was wrong with her son. She had already taken me to many child psychiatrists with no solutions except for them suggesting better parenting techniques. In desperation, she contacted the Royal Children's Hospital, which is the major children's hospital in Australia—the same hospital that had saved my life in 1984 when I was in intensive care with chronic asthma. Her initial contact was a senior physician at the Centre for Adolescent Health. He was not an expert on ADD/ADHD, but he referred me to another child psychiatrist. This time we were getting somewhere. Every week for months, we went to the Children's Hospital to see my new doctor. At first I didn't like going because he asked probing personal questions, but at the same time he understood me a lot better than anyone had before. He placed me on stimulant medication, or Ritalin. My behavior did not change immediately, in fact it didn't change much for about three to four years. This is really what this book is all about.

I have ADHD and I had to learn to live with it. I had to learn to modify my behavior and retrain the way my brain works. Medications help, but they did not resolve my impulsiveness, anger, lack of concentration, and frantic bursts of activity followed by long periods of laziness. I had to learn how to control myself, because I couldn't keep taking Ritalin all the time to modify my behavior. I would rather be unmedicated for the rest of my life than be medicated day in and day out. Most parents and doctors don't really understand how it feels to be knocked out by this medication for days on end. Doctors believe that it is perfectly safe to be on this medication for long periods of time, and I am sure it is. But I would like to know what the studies show on the mental strain of having a hyperstimulated thought process for months and even years on end. I believe that these drugs work best when you use them in moderation. What I mean by this is that you should use them only when you need to. What is the point of medicating your child if he just sits there watching television in an unnatural zombie state?

This is the letter my doctor wrote to the physician to thank him for referring me as a patient.

June 4, 1994

Thank you for referring the above named. I saw Benjamin Polis with his parents on two occasions. Benjamin has a long history of behavior problems. At present there is severe family disharmony because of Ben's behavior. The parents felt they could no longer cope.

When reviewing the history, there was good evidence that Benjamin suffers from attention deficit hyperactivity disorder. At present, the main difficulty is his impulsiveness.

During an individual interview, Benjamin was cooperative. He was fidgety. No evidence of anxiety or depressive disorder. He felt very negative toward his father but was willing to cooperate with treatment.

I have started cognitive behavioral therapy to help Ben. Because of the urgency of this situation, I think combining the use of stimulant medication is justified. The parents and Ben are happy with this after discussion. I will start him on low doses of Ritalin and will continue to see him on an outpatient basis.

First Year at Middle School

My sister decided that I should be sent to a different middle school than hers. She was embarrassed to have me as her brother and did not want to have any social contact with me. I don't blame her for this, because I did not have the best reputation in the area. My name did and still does follow me everywhere I go, but I don't mind. In fact, I get a real kick out of telling people what I am doing now and seeing their faces change when I tell them I'm in college. Whenever people ask, "Whatever happened to that wild son of yours?" both my parents take great pride in telling people who had labeled me a loser all those years ago that I am in college. My mother also finds it quite funny when mothers ask her what I am doing and she tells them.

First year was most probably the worst year of my life. Once again, I hated the school and the school hated me. This was the first time I started to feel totally embarrassed about having attention deficit hyperactivity disorder. My mother told the school of my medical condition, hoping to get a little bit of understanding when I played up. I openly admit that in first year I was completely out of control. I failed every subject with flying colors!

Looking back on it now, I believe there is a good reason for my behavior and dismal academic record. In primary school, everything was regimented. Being told when to sit and when to stand up is perfect for a child like me. However, at middle school this routine was gone. I had to organize myself to get up in time and catch a train and a bus. When I did finally get to school—usually late—I then had to get my books and find my class. In middle school, you change classrooms every period. I forgot books, homework, sports clothes, and so on and continually drew unwanted attention to myself because I was totally disorganized. This is why I believe that if your child does have ADD/ADHD you must train him in primary school to learn to become more independent, better organized at school and home, and to take care of himself. If you do not, he will be overwhelmed by the lack of routine in secondary school and his academic progress and behavior will suffer.

This is exactly what happened to me. One day in a French class we were taking a test, and I couldn't answer even the first question. I think it was how do you say "My name is Ben" in French. I sat there thinking, I am so dumb! I wish I had remembered how to say this sentence in French because I met this hot French girl once and it would have come in handy. After five minutes of just sitting, boredom set in. Like any other ADD/ADHD child, I started to amuse myself by annoying the person next to me, then the teacher. I asked if I could shut the windows because it was cold, which it was not. I climbed up onto the windowsill to shut the top window. Everyone was looking at me and I love an audience. So I pretended to fall! As I was falling, I grabbed the roof rafter and swung back and forward a couple of times. I then pretended to fall again, but this time I did fall and accidentally kicked a boy in the head. In trouble again! The teacher yelled at the top of her lungs, "Go to C3!"—the time-out room.

I don't know why they didn't just send me there permanently, since I spent most of the year there. In the past couple of years, I have spoken to a number of my fellow students from that time and they all say the same thing: "I loved going to C3 because you were always there and would amuse me." In the time-out room we had to write in a book what we had done wrong. These students said they loved to read the C3 book. It was a detailed record of all the things I had done, a record of all the less memorable achievements of my life.

During first year I faced my first challenge in taking medication. Every morning my mother made my breakfast. Neatly laid out was food, Ritalin, asthma tablets, and two types of asthma inhalers. This was my daily routine. It didn't worry me that I had to do this every day. It has been a part of my life since I was eight. The way I see it, I need to take asthma medication every day so I don't die, so there is no difference in taking Ritalin to stop people wanting me to die. That's a joke!

The problem was my lunchtime dose—I didn't take it! This was a big problem during school—even in sixth year. My mother put the Ritalin in a small film canister with my lunch, because I was embarrassed to be taking medication. If anyone asked what the tablet was for, I said it was for asthma. At school I developed such a sneaky technique of taking my Ritalin at lunchtime that people never even saw me take it when I was taking it right in front of them. My friends always used to take my drink from my schoolbag and it used to annoy me, because then I had no liquid to swallow my tablets. It is pretty hard taking tablets with water from a water fountain. In theory, this routine should have worked, but often it didn't. After being confined in a classroom for a couple of hours I was like a caged bull. When the bell went I would burst out of the classroom and hit the school yard to burn off energy. It was time to run, play, and sometimes fight.

Claims that Ritalin suppresses the appetite are pretty much true in my case. Because of Ritalin's side effects, I rarely ate lunch. Although that's not 100 percent correct. When I take Ritalin, I lose my appetite for normal food, such as the lunch my mother made for me. I would often buy more exciting things from the cafeteria and in doing so, I'd forget or not bother to take my medication. This side effect of Ritalin is somewhat strange. I feel hungry because I am weak and have hunger pains, but I won't eat. I eat a little, but I find myself picking at my food and often either throw it out or give it away. The consequences of missing my lunchtime medication usually resulted in my behavior becoming erratic and uncontrollable in afternoon classes.

I Don't Like Being Different!

While at the school I had my first experience of everyone knowing what was wrong with me. A girl had an eating disorder—well, I thought she had an eating disorder. I'm not quite sure but at the time, if I thought something, then to me it was true. I teased her about this and told everyone. I thought she was just doing it to get attention. The student counselor advised the girl to say, when I next said something to her, "Well, I know what is wrong with you!" She did, and I was so angry, I came home and went ballistic at my mother. I told her I didn't want the school to know because this was exactly what I had thought would happen—my embarrassing secret was out. However, I was wrong. The school had not told the girl what was wrong with me. My parents, the school counselor, the girl involved, and I had a meeting. Before then she didn't know that I had ADD/ADHD but now she did, and from then on the whole school knew. From that day, both teachers and students treated me differently. Instead of me being the one picking on other kids, they now had a powerful weapon to use against me, and they did. If I teased someone he threw it back in my face. But, hey, I probably deserved it! Parents must take this possibility into account when they tell people that their son has ADD/ADHD.

The child already feels different and has low self-esteem. If his peers yell, "He's got ADD/ADHD!" his self-esteem and self-perception are further lowered. But if you don't tell the school, how will the school and teachers understand your child's behavior and specific needs? I suggest telling the school after you have stressed that only the teachers are to know. Do not tell the parents of your son's peer group, unless you trust the parents of your son's friends. People talk and people can be very nasty. You must remember that your son does not want to be different but realizes that he is. By telling everyone, you create a bigger problem for him.

Teachers are not trained to deal with students who have ADD/ADHD. They often try ludicrous strategies that do not work and force the affected student to use them. For example, one teacher gave me a rubber band and every time I did something impulsive I was to flick it around my wrist to remind me to control myself. I tried this, but it did nothing for my impulsivity. It was just another tool to amuse myself with in class. I had an unlimited supply, even though I lost them all the time. Every time I was bored or lacked concentration, I flicked the student next to me or shot the rubber band across the room and hit someone. One of my teachers was sick and tired of giving me individual rubber bands, so she decided to give me a massive bag of them. This gave me an unlimited arsenal to fire at people on the bus or out of the bus, people walking to the train station or on the train; and when I was home, I had my family and pets to fire at. You would think that the teachers would have taken the rubber bands away because of their ineffectiveness. But no, I had to keep wearing the rubber band, ridiculous as it was.

If something does not work with your child, try something else. It is for reasons such as this I decided to undertake the challenge of writing this book.

Letters to Parents and First Term Report Card

Dear Mr. and Mrs. Polis,

I am writing to inform you about some behavior of Ben's that I felt you would want to know about. It was brought to my attention that Ben has been telling jokes to other students, the nature of which could be only termed as offensive.

Recently I held a discussion with Ben and some other students about their using language that would fit into the category of sexist terminology. While Ben was not the only one involved it was very clearly impressed upon him that such behavior is totally unacceptable.

Given the nature of the "jokes" Ben has been telling and that some were directed toward female students it would appear he has disregarded my warning. Ben has been constantly advised about more appropriate ways to behave toward fellow students, but he does experience difficulty in following such advice. In order to better monitor Ben's behavior I will be placing him on a conduct card. Staff will be asked to write a descriptive comment on his card for each lesson. Ben should present this card at home each night for you to read and sign.

As a consequence of his telling of jokes of an unacceptable nature, I will restrict Ben to one area of the school for one week. My aim in doing this is to make the point to him that if he cannot control his behavior in an appropriate manner, he will be observed. Hopefully, he will come to see that in order to move freely around the school he must adopt a more responsible approach.

Could I ask that you telephone me at the school so that we can discuss this matter further? My apologies for sending such a long, handwritten letter, but I did want this to reach home today.

Thank you for your support in this matter,

First year coordinator

December 9, 1994

Dear Mr. and Mrs. Polis,

Unfortunately on Friday December 9, Ben was involved in a fighting incident at school. The consequence of this action is that Ben will be suspended from Monday, December 12, to Wednesday, December 14 (three days).

The school has a policy of no fighting and, as this is Ben's
second offense, he has been suspended for three days. If you
have any queries regarding this matter don't hesitate to contact
me at school.

Yours faithfully,
First year coordinator

General Comments from Report Card

Music: Ben is continually calling out, attention seeking, and disrupting the class.

French: Ben has not focused on his work even when redirected to it. His assignment is mostly up-to-date, but other work has been neglected.

English: Ben has indicated that he does have some ability in this area. Inconsistency works against Ben, and until he adopts strategies and listens to advice offered aimed at helping him, he will not gain the best possible outcomes.

The first term report card is all I have from first year. I was meant to get my final report card, however it was not to be. Let me tell you why. By the end of first year I had had enough of middle school and they had had enough of me. School had finished for the year and I had not yet picked up my report card. My mother and I were going shopping, and on our way there we decided to pick up my report card and books from my locker. At the front office I asked to see the first year coordinator. She said, "Who do you think you are, arriving at school without an appointment, out of uniform, et cetera?" I told her the school year was finished, therefore I did not have to wear a uniform, I just wanted my report and would then leave. She told me I would have to wait until three o'clock, about two hours. I replied that I wanted it now because my mother was waiting. She said my mother would have to wait and I would have to sit in the office for the two hours and wait. I was not going to play her game, so I told her that she could keep my report card and walked off to get my books from the locker. She stood there and yelled at the top of her lungs, "Benjamin Polis! Come back here! You are not going anywhere!" She followed me to my locker and again demanded that I wait. I did not say a word. She had no control over me, she knew. I loved it! I didn't care. I was going to another school the following year and her threats did not matter. With my books, I walked out of that school with her still following me and still yelling, jumped into my mother's car, and we drove off. I did not care then and still don't care now. I was glad to be out of the school and have not been back since. As I said at the start of this chapter, first year was probably the worst year of my life—academically, mentally, and socially, not to mention behaviorally.

Camp Chaos

During the summer holidays my mother sought peace and quiet by sending me to a Christian camp. It was established for underprivileged children whose parents could not afford a vacation for them, along with many others just there to have a good time. After the disaster of my first year in middle school, I was mentally unstable and very angry.

On the second day of camp I lost control totally. I was quietly sitting on my bunk when another boy started hitting me with a broomstick, just to get a reaction. He got one, all right! I grabbed the broomstick and repeatedly smashed it over him, yelling at the top of my lungs, "How do you like it, *bitch*?" The leader, who was much older and stronger, finally restrained me. My impulsive behavior and temper were out of control.

The following day a girl started teasing me about bashing someone with a broomstick. I told her, "F*@# off! You're just a stupid fat cow!" She hit me in the face. I lost it again. With one almighty swing I knocked her out! I'm not proud of this, especially because she was a girl. However, an angry and impulsive boy with ADD/ADHD does not think about what he is doing and doesn't understand why he is doing it. I now know why I was so mentally unstable then. I hated myself and I hated everyone else. My parents had sent me away like some kind of condemned criminal. I didn't want to go to the stupid camp and I hated everyone there. But most of all I hated myself. I was about to go to my fifth school at the age of thirteen. I felt that no one liked me, and now even my family couldn't handle me. Along with this, I was in an unfamiliar environment. My ordered routine was not there, and I didn't have my mother to do everything for me. Camps and I don't really work well. As a matter of fact, my mother always had to drive back after a few days and pick me up from almost every camp I went to. She liked the thought of me going away, but she hated it because she always knew that she would have to come back in about three days to pick me up.

The funny thing is that at this camp I met one of my best friends. His name is Jared Smith. He was really sick and lay in bed with a cold for about five days. He was obviously bored and wanted some stimulation. As he got better he thought he would have a go at setting me up. Not a good idea! I don't remember exactly what happened, but I do remember what I did. I jumped on top of him as he lay in bed and punched the crap out of him! So if you look at my stats, the camp went for five days and I knocked out three people in five days. Not bad! Later I will tell you how Jared and I became friends.

Another example of a camp not going down too well was my first year camp. This camp was absolutely wild. The teachers' camp was about half a mile away from the students'. The students were meant to sleep in these old trains converted into dorms. However, no one slept! If you can imagine about a hundred and fifty kids running wild at about three in the morning, jumping on top of the trains, and just being foolish, that was camp. However, it was during this camp I had my first experience with a girl. It is pretty funny looking back on it now. See, I was set up with this girl, like you are in first year, and we had to kiss. I had never kissed a girl before and didn't have a clue. Well, anyway, we started to kiss and she didn't stop. The problem was it was cold outside and I had a bit of asthma. I breathe through my mouth like a lot of asthmatics, and when this girl was kissing me I couldn't breathe. I pulled away and started to cough. I think I am the only person in the world to have an asthma attack from kissing.

But this is not why I got into trouble. The girl and I slept in the same bed that night, but nothing happened sexually. Anyway, the following morning she told the first year coordinator, "I slept with Ben Polis last night." Well, the coordinator misunderstood. We were sent home that day. My mother once again had to come and pick me up. We were both made examples of because the teachers were so angry that all the students had been out partying the night before. I didn't really mind being sent home anyway—the camp was crap! When my mother came to pick me up she was so angry. On the way home she wouldn't even buy me a McDonald's hamburger when she bought my sister one. I was in *so* much trouble again!

What to Look for in a Camp

Even though I had a bad experience with camps I believe they can be very beneficial to an ADD/ADHD child or teenager. I believe the reason I had such bad experiences with camps was because I was so mentally unstable at that time of my life. Also, every time I was sent away by my mum it was because she was trying to get rid of me on school breaks.

Camps can play a very valuable role in building better self-esteem and self-perception in young people. Camps often promote teamwork and a better understanding of other people's needs.

Along with this they often promote physical activity and are full of excitement—just what an ADD/ADHD kid needs. Parents often send kids away on school break, which is a great idea because it allows a break between school and school holidays. If your child has a bad school break and finds himself in trouble he will take this into the next term. It is harder for him to get into trouble when he is in the controlled environment of a camp.

Also, if your son has trouble making friends he should find it easier at camp because of the closeness camps promote. And for parents, when your child is at camp you have a much needed break, too.

Second Year: Catholic School

My mother chose my next school and she did well. The criteria she used were simple but quite brilliant. The school had to be small enough so that I got the necessary attention that I was lacking at larger schools. An all-boys school was also very important to limit distractions. I am eternally grateful that she found this school.

I believe this was the best school I have been to out of a possible five other candidates. The reason was very simple. It was a small Catholic school of around four hundred boys. It only went from first to fourth year, which allowed a lot of personal attention for students both capable and not so capable. I believe the big difference between this school and the other schools I attended was that the teachers simply cared a lot more about their students. Discipline was enforced and you really couldn't get away with a lot because everyone knew everyone. It did not matter if you were in first year, it was quite acceptable to hang out with fourth year students. I had never been to a school such as this. The school also had a very diverse cultural base of students. Again, it did not matter where you were from. Prejudices did not arise.

This school was perfect for me. Unlike other schools where you had to move from classroom to classroom, here the teachers came to you. Some students may not like this idea, but I think it is fantastic. You had the same desk and sat next to the same person every day, all day. You had your own personal space, which was yours for the whole year, according to unwritten class rules. This is especially great for an ADD/ADHD child because your own personal space allows you to settle in and get off to a great start. At the previous school, if I forgot a book I had to put my hand up and ask permission to go get it from my locker. This annoyed the teachers. Then I had to run to my locker and back so I wouldn't fall behind in the class period. However, at my new school, if I forgot a book all I had to do was get it from my in-room locker. That's what I call efficiency. I feel that the school's greatest attribute was not that it was small, or even that it had a great academic record, but that it gave kids a second and third chance and persisted with troubled students. The school had many students who had been expelled from other schools. Unlike other schools that shifted the problem on, they took the time to resolve the problem.

For the first time in my school life, I decided to adopt a new radical plan. I was going to try! At first I hated going to the new school. However, I liked it better than my previous one. No one knew me and I could start off fresh—and I did. I tried hard, I behaved, and I did homework for the first time in my life. But this smoke screen was soon pulled aside. Jared Smith blew my cover! He was the same boy I had bashed at the Christian camp only a couple of months earlier. I did not remember him, or even remember bashing him, until he confronted me one day at school. I didn't have any friends at the time and I remember talking to a Down syndrome student named Paul on my first day. Jared was also a new student in second year and was in the same position as I. However, he had made friends a lot easier than me at first. The reason I had not made any friends was not lack of social skills. It was due to the new Ben, the quiet and settled Ben. I lay low for the first couple of weeks and did not intrude on anyone. Then Jared opened his big mouth!

When he confronted me a couple of weeks into the first term I remember exactly what he said: "Are you Ben Polis from—?"

"No, of course not!" I replied with a cheeky grin. My cover was blown big-time. We became good friends from that day forward. A couple of weeks later he told me that he had seen me on the first day and crapped himself and walked the other way. He told me that he couldn't believe his eyes, thinking to himself, A new school and I am stuck with a psycho! I had not realized that he had already been telling people that I was a little crazy and that I had beaten up half the camp! I guess this is the reason no one wanted to be my friend. After a while, people realized that I wasn't crazy and they all wanted to talk to me. I guess they were intrigued by the stories Jared had told them, and soon I made heaps of friends.

It was during second year that I uncovered a gift that I hadn't really used. I had always been a great athlete in primary school but didn't really think much of it because I was only competing against my fellow students. The annual athletics day was coming up and I was pretty cocky that I would win. Like all things, I guess, in life, I have this idea that I am the best even if I am not. This allows me to believe in myself. I had already sorted out my competition, Tim Prescott, the fastest kid in second year. I had challenged him verbally in school. I said I was going to kill him on the running track. This went down very well. A bit of rivalry from the new kid to knock off the reigning champion was just what I needed to make a name for myself. The big day came, and Melbourne turned on the weather the way only Melbourne can—it rained and the athletics day was washed out. The school rescheduled it, and the Melbourne weather turned on again. It rained harder than last time. The showdown we were waiting for was not going to happen.

The school athletics day is how kids qualify for the inter-school athletics day. The problem was that I had had no opportunity to qualify. So Tim was chosen for all the events based on his previous year's performance. I made a stink over this, and I was allowed to run the two hundred meters in the interschool athletics championships. This was not taken well by the other students. Who does this new kid think he is, telling his new school that he is running in the two hundred meters? I didn't care—I put on an image of invincibility.

The big day came. I borrowed my mate Jared's spikes, since I didn't have any, having never run in a proper athletics meet before. They were about two sizes too small. People would not have known it, but I was scared. I had convinced this new school that I was the best thing since sliced bread. But I didn't even know if I could win! It was make-or-break time. I was either going to be a hero or be labeled a loser like I had been at my old middle school. I was determined to win at any cost!

I lined up in the blocks with the whole school watching me.

Because it was such a small school all the students and teachers were allowed to come and cheer us on. The starter's gun fired! Bang! Oh, no! I had false started! I guess that was my impulsiveness shining through. I lined up again, but this time I started perfectly. I ran like I had never run before. I remember going into the eighty-meter bend coming about third. When I got around the last bend, and with about another eight meters to go, I was in front by about two meters. The whole school cheered me on! Spurred on by this, I increased my lead even more. I couldn't see any of the other runners—I had left them for dead. I finished in first place with my arms up in the air like Michael Johnson at the Atlanta Olympic Games. I won by a huge margin—about seven meters! I had done it! I had believed I could and I did!

After I finished I was approached by one of the marshals. At the time I was talking to the school principal. The marshal asked me, "Do you run?"

Yes, but only from my mum! I thought. I then replied, "No, I have never run before for a club."

"Well, you should—you nearly broke the interschool record." She took down my phone number and my running career was started. I ran straight to a public phone to call my mum. I told her what I had achieved. She was so pleased! I'm not sure if she was most pleased at me winning or that for the first time in my entire schooling life I was finally happy!

After I had finished talking to my mother I went and sat with the other students. I was suddenly being approached by teachers, parents, and students, all congratulating me on my performance. I then asked—no that's not true, I demanded—to be allowed to choose other events that I wanted to compete in. I then went on to win the 100 meter, 400 meter, high jump, javelin, and the 4 × 100 meter relay. Our second year athletic team won the championship for their year level, thanks to me! The following day I went to school and people kept congratulating me! I loved it! The only downside was I had created a nickname for myself that I was not too fond of—Roids! There was a rumor going around the school that I was on steroids. How pathetic! Would you believe that a fourteen-year-old boy would be doing steroids? Hello, it was not East Germany!

I sailed through second year with average marks. No real trouble or anything too alarming. For the first time in my whole life I had found a school that accepted me, and I started to love going to school. My behavior at home improved greatly and my bursts of anger became less frequent.

It's strange when you think about it. Parents are always asking, Why is their son acting in such an abnormal manner? However, from my personal experience, I believe as a parent you must look at your son's environment. If he has low self-esteem because he can't read like the other students, gets into trouble, and can't make friends because he is not accepted because of his erratic behavior, you must resolve these issues first if you want to improve your son's behavior. I believe that people who fight and are angry do so because they are unhappy with their own perception of themselves. When I was younger, I got into fights in and out of school. But when I was happy, these ADHD symptoms were not as dominant—just something to think about in your own child's environment.

My report card from second year showed some great improvements in my academic and behavioral performance—especially when you compare it to my performance in first year when I didn't pass one subject. Second year was a real growth period for me. It was during this time that I started to learn the foundations of my many self-help techniques, which I will discuss in Part Two. Another important fact that I learned in second year was that self-esteem and basically just feeling good about yourself really contribute to overall improvements in behavior. This is even more important to an ADD/ADHD child. An unhappy ADD/ADHD child will always make everyone else around him unhappy. So again it is fundamentally important to look at your child's social environment.

Third Year:
Bad Boy Ben Is Back!

Move over, first year—third year was without a doubt my worst school year. It really didn't make sense since I had had such a fantastic year in second year. My grades had improved; I even passed all my subjects for the first time in my life. My behavior was nearly perfect—well, as perfect as an ADD/ADHD child's behavior can be. So, you might be wondering, what the hell happened in a couple of months? You'd better hang on to your seats because my life is about to get ugly!

Third year started like every other year. Each school year begins with an assembly, where your coordinators lecture you for hours about the same thing every year: "This is one of the most important years of your school life and you must make a more concentrated effort with your studies! Blah, blah, blah!" Well, unlike the year before, I *had* now made a concentrated decision not to take my studies, or life in general, seriously. This is not something that I recommend to anyone. The only thing I successfully achieved in third year was to successfully *mess up* my life!

Again, as in first year, I was out of control. However, there was a big difference between first and third year. In first year I didn't know any better. I was always like that and I had come to the conclusion that I was out of control and I could not change that. But this time I was out of control because I had deliberately chosen to be. I knew I could behave and be an asset to my school and society. I had done it and I had done it all by myself without anyone else's help. I had no secret pill that changed me into a perfect student. The only secret I had uncovered was self-control. I had chosen to take control of my behavior and subsequently my life. I like to refer to this as, I was in control of my brain instead of my brain controlling me. However, in third year I chose to let my erratic brain control me once again.

I believe this thought process and change in my behavior was the result of a number of factors. I had become a parent's worst nightmare. I was a fifteen-year-old, rebellious know-it-all. I was rebelling against everyone and everything. Authority was my archenemy and I was determined to crush it! But this was not to be. Authority won in a quick and decisive battle. So if I can paint a picture of myself, at the time I had very dangerous personality traits.

I was:

impulsive
angry
a smart-ass
conceited
extremely violent

very intelligent
manipulative
horny teenager controlled by my crotch
rebellious

As you can see, I was again my own worst enemy. It was not my ADHD, it was my way of thinking. My ADHD only exaggerated my very dangerous personality traits. I lasted only about five weeks into the term before I was suspended. I was in a fight with an older boy in fourth year. I gave him a beating, though. I guess, looking back on it now, I was not fighting him because I didn't like him. I had a point to prove. I wanted to be *bad*! This extremely aggressive and self-destructive attitude of mine followed me everywhere I went. I got into fights at school, while coming home from school, on the weekends, and at home. My answer to all my problems was to do what I do best—be impulsive, which often meant fighting.

By this time the school had had enough of me. I was put on probation and got a daily report card. This report card is a good idea. It is also an excellent idea for parents with children who have ADD/ADHD. How it works is quite simple. In every class your son gets a report card with comments from the teacher. Then he brings the card home for you to read and sign. It gives a running commentary on your son's daily life.

When thinking about third year I always tell people of my love-hate relationship with my math teacher. He hated me and I loved him hating me! He had a very distinctive voice, which I could mimic perfectly. Every time he yelled at me I replied in his voice. "Yes, Mr. ——!" It made him go wild. My fellow students loved it because it was so funny. But the strange thing about this relationship between him and me was that we shared an unspoken language: I knew what he was thinking and he knew what I was thinking. My math class always went like this: I had one warning before I was kicked out of the class. But I was not told verbally that I had been given a warning, it was just a look and I knew that look. When I did something else disruptive, there was no yelling or anything else said then, either. I knew it and he knew it. He then walked over to my desk as cool as a cucumber and got on one side of it. I got on the other side and we carried my desk outside together. But, remember, this was all done without speaking. The students laughed because it worked like clockwork, and it happened every lesson.

It was during third year that I started to experiment with alcohol and marijuana. Now this is a tip for all parents out there. All kids experiment with booze and drugs. If you decide to turn a blind eye to this you are only encouraging it. If you think it's hard for your child to get booze, it's not. But the surprising thing is that kids can often get drugs more easily than booze. There is no age limit for buying drugs; you don't have to be twenty-one. The only thing you need is money! I started to experiment with marijuana. I even attempted to grow some. I realized there was a demand and someone needed to supply it, so that was going to be me!

At the time, my mother teased me because my marijuana plants always died. We lived on the beach, and she told me it was the salt from the sea that was killing my plants. So I tried again and again with the same result. I then thought there is no salt inside, so that's where I'll grow my plants. Dad came home from work one night and went into his shed to get a beer. He discovered that all the shed lights were missing. The first place he looked was my room. To his very angry surprise he found his lights in my walk-in closet cleverly hooked up to a timer I had bought. Mum and Dad let me keep growing my babies, but like the ones outside these plants died, too. It was around this time that I gave up on supplying. I never had anything to supply! A few years later I found out why my plants never grew. My mum told me, as she laughed uncontrollably, that she had killed my plants. She said that since I was going to try to grow them anyway, she could protect me by controlling them. She killed them just before it was time to harvest them.

Anyway, that's not my point. If you look at the personality traits I had at the time and then add a combination of drugs and alcohol, you have yourself a recipe for disaster.

I remember one night very clearly. It was a Friday night and a couple of friends and I were smoking pot in my bedroom. My mother came in and could smell it. She went ballistic, screaming and yelling at me. She told the other boys that she was going to call their mothers. This triggered something in my head and I went absolutely crazy! I kicked the front door in and swore the most vulgar of profanities at my mother. I walked out the front gate with my father in pursuit. I turned around and picked up an extremely heavy flowerpot and threw it at him. He moved in the nick of time, and it exploded on impact. My mum has since asked me to move a similar flowerpot and I can't do it.

My friends and I walked to the closest train station. My father had jumped into his car and was following us. He caught up with us about fifty meters from the train station. He pulled over next to me and told me to get into the car. I ran up and started to punch my father in the head through the driver's side window. I kicked the driver's side door in. I then ran off with my friends as if nothing had happened. The following day my father tried to get a restraining order on me. My mother would not let him go through with it. I don't understand how it would have worked anyway, because we both live under the same roof. My dad always comes up with great ideas like that.

I am certainly not proud of this and it seems unbelievable when I think about it today. However, it happened and I did do it. I could leave things out of this book that I am embarrassed about, such as this, but they happened and I did them. It was a part of my life, and I don't believe that the truth should be manipulated to cover my embarrassment. I have thought about this incident a number of times since. I do not put it down to having ADHD. For some reason unknown to me, when I use marijuana it makes me crazy. I have discussed this with other ADD/ADHD people and they also believe this to be true. Marijuana, I believe without any scientific proof, should not be the drug of choice for an ADD/ADHD person or any person. It makes you go crazy without you even realizing it.

I believe marijuana should be legalized for medical purposes, for example, for people with cancer or AIDS. However, I strongly recommend that if you or your child have ADHD, you should stay clear of it.

During third year I constantly challenged my boundaries at school. I was on probation and I decided that I would not change my ways. I continued causing trouble at school and fighting. The school had had enough this time. I was playing Australian Rules football at lunchtime. It was a favorite pastime there. Quite often we played with fifty plus kids from all the years. It was quite funny, though. The cultural diversity meant most of the boys did not have a clue how to play. We had Vietnamese boys, Greeks, Italians, Yugoslavians, Cambodians, etc. So we played a game that resembled more a Roman battle at the Coliseum. Rough and tough were basically the only rules. When someone was tackled and brought to the ground, the call would go out! "Stakes on!" You would have anywhere from ten to thirty boys jumping on someone. It was great!

Anyway, on this day I was dominating the game as usual, kicking goals and playing as roughly as I could. I was playing on a new boy who had a bit of a name as a good footballer. I didn't think much of him and was outmarking him at every opportunity. He didn't like this. It all got a bit heated, as it did during these games. Well, he and I had been sizing each other up for months. We had a small fight, nothing over-the-top. But the only thing the teacher on duty saw was me swing as hard as I could and hit him in the jaw. I was suspended once again, but this time it was very different. The school called my father and me up to the school at the end of the day. I was told that I had to find a new school. I burst into tears, I couldn't believe it—they were serious this time. I loved it there, it was the best school I had ever attended, and I never thought they would really expel me! I was told to try to find a new school and if I couldn't I was to call them. The school insisted that *I* was to find the new school, not my parents. I did try to find a new school but no one wanted me—funny about that! Anyway, I had already been to all the schools in my area and this school was about a forty-minute train ride away.

Mum jokes about it today, saying things like, "I thought you would end up going to school on the other side of Melbourne!"

The school was very dear to my heart and I was not going to let them throw me out. I had a real change of heart. I finally realized that I had been biting the hand that fed me. I wrote the following letter to the school, pleading to be reinstated as a student:

To Mr. ——,

I have thought about my actions leading up to my suspension (being asked to leave). I have come to the conclusion that I have not been acting in an appropriate way to my teachers. I know now that I should have treated them with more respect and listened to what they have been saying over the past couple of months. I would like to come back and try to become a better student than I have been in the past.

Yours sincerely,
Benjamin Polis

Here is the letter the school sent me in reply.

September 17, 1996

Dear Mr. and Mrs. Polis,

Following our conversation, the school is prepared to allow Ben to continue his education here next term under the following conditions:

It is required that Ben give an undertaking not to be involved or associated with any form of intimidation, bullying, verbal or physical harassment of any member of this school community, student or staff. As a member of the school community, his conduct with the general public must be appropriate.

Ben will be on probation for the remainder of this year. It is our present intention that in the middle of next term, a meeting will take place, at which his academic progress and conduct will be discussed. If satisfactory progress has been made, Ben's position will be reviewed.

Any involvement in the activities mentioned above, which come to the school's attention, will result in Ben's position being reviewed, and you may be asked to withdraw Ben from the school.

This letter is to be signed by you, the parents, and Ben himself and returned at the start of next term.

Yours sincerely,

———

Principal

As you can see, the school did give me another chance once again. I could not find another school that would accept me. The strict rules above on my reinstatement were very hard to keep. I was not allowed to come back until the next year, in fourth year. During third year I was suspended for over two months altogether, on about eight different occasions. I would again like to thank the school for giving me a last chance after many previous chances. Likewise, I would like to highlight the tremendous support the school offers to students like me.

I only recently found out why I was not accepted into any other schools. My third year coordinator had called all the other Catholic schools in the area and told them not to let me in. He was using some very clever reverse psychology. I guess it worked.

My report card from third year was not very good, as you can imagine. I will not bore you with the details, but it went a little bit like this:

English: Due to Ben's many absences, it is difficult to accurately assess him in this subject. When work is submitted it is of a very good standard, and reflects considerable thought, but it is often late and therefore marked as such. He needs to improve his organizational skills and submit work on time.

A disappointing effort!

Looking back on my report card from third year made me realize something that I had not understood until recently. All my report card grades for class work were extremely poor, often Fs and Ds. However, my test grades were in the high nineties. It seems a bit strange, but not for an ADHD student. The problem is quite simple. In class I cannot concentrate due to the distracting environment. But when I take an exam, I can concentrate because of the settled environment. So does this mean that I have selective concentration difficulties? Do I think so? No, I *know* so! Just something to think about with your child's education. Maybe you should look at his school environment in closer detail. You may see a huge improvement.

At age sixteen I was also accused of burning down a local Australian Rules football club. I remember the day very clearly. It was seven o'clock in the morning and Mum woke me up to tell me the police were at the front door. Six detectives in black trench coats confronted me. Someone had told them that I had burned down the local football club. This is just another example of my bad reputation. I had not done it but the police were sure I had. I eventually proved my innocence because I'd been at work when it happened. But I learned something from all this. I can now see why people who are innocent of a crime confess. When all this was happening, for a little while, the police actually convinced me that I was guilty. But I stuck to my guns and told them that if they thought I had done it, it was their job to prove it! They never did, and I thank God that He made me a strong enough person so that I did not give in to the massive pressure I was under.

Fourth Year

During fourth year nothing really changed much. I was still Ben Polis and I was still acting like the class clown. I was not as bad as I had been in third year, but there was not much change. However, there was one very important difference. This time I was on probation. Any false move and I was out. Having this threat constantly over my head did deter me somewhat. It was during fourth year that I found out that I had some very strong allies. The first was my third year English and drama teacher. She had constantly stuck her neck out in my defense in third year. But I did not have her in the fourth to mother me, as she had in the third. Still, in fourth year I was not alone. My home-room teacher was the best teacher I have ever had. I found out in fourth year that the school had wanted me to leave, but he had bravely volunteered to be my homeroom and English teacher. Without the support of these two teachers I feel my life would not have turned out the way it has today. Thank you!

Here is a letter Mark Stracey sent when I told him I was writing this book.

May 30, 2001

When you enter the teaching profession, nobody warns you about the multitude of personalities that you will confront, day in, day out. It's strange how, over the years, you remember certain students: the bright one, the funny one, the rude one, the challenging one, and the poetic one. . . . Ben Polis was all of these.

I was only in my second year of teaching when I learned that Ben was going to be in my class. An involuntary shudder passed through my body. Ben was the loud one in the yard. Restless, energetic, the ringleader, exhausting, confronting. In short, Ben was hard work.

Sometimes when you teach, you have to get beyond (or beneath? or through?) the disruptive behavior and get to know the individual. Although there were times when Ben could be maddening—what fifteen-year-old isn't?—I got to know him. It was worth the effort. Ben could give the impression that he was uninterested, disorganized, and a disaster waiting to happen. In truth, there thrived a keen intellect, an ability to think clearly, and an articulate young man.

So how did I cope with Ben?

A lot of it was trial and error. I tried a variety of teaching strategies and approaches, sometimes in consultation with Ben. I certainly learned a lot through having Ben in my classes.

In order to keep Ben engaged, tasks had to be short, sharp, and hands-on. For instance, when teaching essay structures, Ben didn't cope with the simple chalk-and-talk approach. He showed real progress, however, when he could cut an essay up into its constituent parts, label them, and use them as a model for his own writing.

In a similar way, Ben responded to visual and aural stimuli. He could, for instance, listen to a piece of music or look at a photo and then write a short piece. The key, it seemed to me, was to break up the lessons, so that he could avoid being bored. The other key was to set clearly defined parameters for him: "We'll listen to a piece of music, then I'd like you to write two stanzas." This worked well for Ben.

It was equally important that Ben learned to work within the guidelines that the rest of the class worked within, hands up, etc. Keeping Ben on task was a battle. At times, he would lose the plot. Perhaps the thing that was most effective, at these times, was giving him choices. "Ben, if you continue to talk and to interrupt the class, I will have to move you to the front," "to write in your diary," "to ask you to leave the room," etc. This allowed Ben to take responsibility for his own actions and the consequences of those actions. The fact that I had built a relationship with him gave me some referential power over him. I tried to ensure that I would criticize his behavior rather than express my disappointment with him. For the most part, this worked well.

When Ben graduated, I was genuinely proud of him. He had worked hard under trying circumstances. There were times when I really wondered if he'd ever make it. It's so wonderful to see the great adult that he has become.

In fourth year my academic performance did improve. I had chosen to do fifth year mathematics in fourth year—which is quite funny because I had failed third year math with flying colors. This was the vice principal's idea to encourage me and relieve some of the boredom I was constantly complaining about at school. It worked quite well. When I am challenged I concentrate better. If something is easy I amuse myself in class, often annoying the teacher with my disruptive behavior.

This is something to think about with your child. If you expect an ADD/ADHD child to sit still with no mental or physical challenge, you have no chance. So you should always have a bag of toys, video games, books, and so on to stimulate your child. This will make your life a bit easier.

My schoolwork did improve, but my behavior did not improve drastically. I was still getting in trouble, but I was not failing as I had in the third year. I often handed in work late because I was so disorganized, but I got it in. This was a problem of mine throughout my whole school life, including my final year.

Below are some letters my parents received from the school.

Dear Mr. and Mrs. Polis,

I am writing to you to let you know that Ben made a very unpleasant comment to me today in my classroom. Ben is no longer actually in my class, he simply walked into it—P6—today.

I am quite a tolerant person with a reasonable sense of humor. I am not averse to a little friendly banter but I am not used to foul remarks, masked as jokes, being directed at me. I was offended and disgusted. I require a written apology from him at least. I will contact you further, next week.

This letter does not tell the entire story. I had been kicked out of the class because of my disruptive behavior, most probably because I was bored. The problem with this disciplinary technique is that it sends you outside to an even more mind-numbing environment. So like any ADHD child I amused myself. I started to approach the other classrooms in the corridor. I pretended to be a door-to-door salesman, selling exercise bikes cheap. The catch was that I had identified all the larger teachers as my target market. But the reason the exercise bikes were so cheap was that they were missing the seats, which I used as a selling point. The seatless exercise bikes offered sexual stimulation to keep you exercising. The students were in hysterics and the teachers were after my head. That's the whole story. But it's funny how teachers always have such a pleasant way of retelling stories to parents.

> *Dear Mr. and Mrs. Polis,*
>
> *Due to poor behavior in the cafeteria over the last few weeks and the showing of disrespect for its manageress, Ben is not allowed to enter the cafeteria for all of next week. He will not be allowed to enter the cafeteria following that until he has passed on to me a letter of apology for her.*
>
> *Fourth year coordinator*

The funny thing about this whole situation was that I got my friends to buy my lunch from the cafeteria and then subsequently ate it in front of the cafeteria lady to try to annoy her. Also, I never wrote that apology, but I probably should have. So here goes.

> *Dear Mrs. ——,*
>
> *I am sorry for my disrespectful behavior directed at you in 1997.*

May 19, 1997

Dear Mr. and Mrs. Polis,

As I indicated in our telephone conversation earlier today,
and after consultation with the principal and the fourth year
coordinator, Ben has been suspended from the school for an
incident which took place on Ventura bus no. 703 on the
morning of Monday, May 19.

The incident concerned an exchange between Ben and a
group of disabled persons who regularly use this bus. A parent
of a student who will be attending the school in 1998 was
most upset and telephoned the school to convey his dismay at
Ben's behavior. It is of concern to us that the image of the
school has been tarnished and Ben's insensitivity to the needs
of disabled persons has been highlighted.

Both the principal and myself hope that Ben realizes that as
he is making decisions for next year, incidents such as today's
may have an impact on the school's willingness to recommend
that Ben continue his education elsewhere in 1998.

Yours sincerely,
Deputy principal

At the bottom of this letter I found a note attached by my father. It states that I was suspended again just before the end of the school year and had to pick up my report card after all the other students had left. This was so I could not incite students into more rebellious behavior.

Well, it was true that I had insulted those disabled passengers on the school bus. However, they had asked for it. These two disabled people were a couple. They were loudmouthed and rude. They were insulting the students of my school. However,

I should have bitten my tongue, which would have gone against all my ADHD impulses. But reading this letter reminded me of something else.

Every time I got on a bus throughout my school life every bus driver knew my name. They would say things like, "Ben, are we going to have a good day today?" I thought this was pretty funny because I had never told them my name. Yet they knew who I was. Along with this, about a year ago a lady on the train said, "Hi, Ben. How have you been?"

I looked at her and said, "Who the hell are you?" She said I didn't know her but she knew me. The lady had caught the same train as me for three years. She told me that she recited my daily routine—of calling out on the train and so on—to her friends at work during morning tea. She also told me that I had developed a cult following in her office and they were bitterly disappointed when I was not on the train. I guess I made their day go a bit faster. Clearly the world would be a very boring place without ADD/ADHD people like me.

August 25, 1997

Mr. and Mrs. Polis,

I am writing to express my growing concern regarding Ben's attitude and behavior in class.

After discussions between your son's teachers and his homeroom teacher, it has become necessary to again inform you of our concerns, particularly Ben's disruptive, antagonistic, intimidating, and at times aggressive behavior in class.

It is of concern to us that Ben's behavior is reflected in his poor attitude to his schoolwork and of greater concern is the effect that your son's behavior is having on other members of

*his class. Every member of the community has the right to
learn. At present Ben is not respecting the right of other
students to learn.*

*The decision has been taken that if Ben's behavior
continues to have a detrimental effect on the learning
environment of the school and other students or is in any way
intimidating to either staff or students, he will be withdrawn
from classes and have no further contact with the student body.
This suspension from classes will be for a period of one or more
days. During this time Ben will be given all work by the class
teacher and will be expected to complete the work.*

*After the period of withdrawal from classes has been served,
and after discussion between you, Ben will be allowed to
resume classes. If Ben's behavior continues to be disruptive,
Ben may be suspended from the school. In this circumstance,
you will be contacted by phone and asked to pick your son up
at the school. He will not return to the school until an
interview is held between your son, yourselves, and myself.*

*At this interview the conditions upon which Ben will be
readmitted to the school will be discussed. If the situation
arises where it is deemed necessary to again suspend Ben from
the school, your son's position here will be reviewed. This letter
is to be signed by you and Ben himself and returned. If you
wish to discuss this matter further, you may contact me at the
school to make an appointment.*

Deputy principal

On a brighter note, I have included some of the poetry that I
completed in fourth year. This shows the academic abilities
about which my teachers so often reminded me, and which I

chose to ignore until I reached my final year of high school. The ironic thing is that I handed in lots of work I did in fourth year in my final year because I was too lazy to do any new work.

You Did the Right Thing (Vietnam War)

This poem is dedicated to my dad, who was conscripted at twenty-one to the Australian Army to fight in Vietnam.

I'm doing the right thing,
I think.
Good vs. Evil,
Bad against good.
I'm a freedom fighter,
I'm a baby killer,
I'm a murderer.
I'm trapped.
Drop a bomb on the Vietcong,
Hope it hits.
Damn, I missed.
What was I thinking?
I must have been pissed,
I just killed a family of six.
Drop another and another,
Till good beats evil.
Bomb by bomb,
Spray by spray,
The nightmares are here to stay.
All I hear in my sleep
Is the scream of the bombs

That made so many people weep.
Too many men fell
In the jungles of hell.
My mates are home,
But the scars are here to stay.
My best mate's in a chair,
But his legs are not there.
Another friend walks with a walker,
Another with a cane.

I have another friend
Who shoots,
Not with a gun,
With a needle,
To escape the Vietnam pain.
They said, "Come on, lads,
Come and help your country,
Come on, do what's right.
Remember, always look down,
Because if that's a mine,
Your legs are gone.
The noise, the fright,
Will echo in your ears for life,
But remember, lads,
You did what's right."

Stop the War!

Stop the war,
I can't handle it no more.
Good men dying,

Can't stop the mothers crying.
Fathers proud,
but nothing can stop the imminent mushroom cloud.
No winners in this amazing game of death and despair.
Where, where is my mate gone!
His wife Beth will soon be told of her love's bloody death.
Politicians sit in their chairs controlling us like pawns.
But do I see those bastards' legs being torn in two?
I think not—what a f*@#ing crock!
Some of these boys seem young enough to be back in their
cots. Stop the war, I can handle it no more. Stop it now,
Because no one is going to stop that bullet . . .
With your name on it!

Kill the Queen

Dedicated to one day see Australia a republic

Kill the queen and be ruled by Mr. Sheen.
He'd do a better job than that pompous snob.
He'd make us laugh not like that silly old fart.
She can't run her kids, so what's going to happen to us?
She made a fuss when the stupid bag fell out of a double-
    decker bus.
She broke her hip in the fall—the media had a ball.
They said they cared but all they wrote about was her
    damn hair.
Get off the throne and let's watch her moan.

No one likes her, no one cares.
Let's assassinate this phoney and her snobbish heirs.

Get her off the throne.
Get her off our money.
Get her out of the palace for which we pay.

Don't throw flowers . . .
Throw grenades in vain . . .
To cause maximum republican pain!

My report card from fourth year is basically the same, with the same comments I have had since I was in primary school. For example: "Ben has the ability to do well in this subject when he applies himself. He is often more interested in attracting attention for himself than concentrating on his work." I noticed something else. The subjects that interested me—such as history, geography, and English to a certain degree—I did exceptionally well in. In history and geography I got straight As, but I failed the subjects where I had little or no interest. For example, in science and woodwork I didn't even hand in one piece of work.

I bet this is true of your own ADD/ADHD child, too. He does exceptionally well at things he enjoys or has an interest in. Conversely, when asked to do simple things like clean his room, it is nearly impossible to get results. There is a very good reason for this. An ADD/ADHD child sees little benefit in doing something that he sees as boring. So the answer is to redirect the child's interests into the classroom. If he has to do a science project on coal production and he has no interest in coal production, I can bet you that he won't do it or he will get a bad grade. But if he likes cars, why don't you speak to the teacher and ask him or her if he can do a research project on cars instead? Some teachers may say, "Well, that's not what we are studying." But I think it would be a lot more beneficial for your child to learn something rather than nothing. The good thing about this is that as your child gets older, he can choose the subjects he wants to study, which allows this to happen a lot more easily.

On a closing note, I loved every minute at that school and it holds some of my best experiences in life. Because the school went up only to fourth year, once again my parents were on the hunt for another school. They found it, the same school that had rejected my plea to attend it only a year before.

To finish up with fourth year, I have included the letter my teacher gave me on my last day. He gave the letters as awards with fitting names on them for each student. I won the award for the student who repeatedly tried to break every school rule and succeeded. This is the letter he wrote to me and it makes me feel good every time I read it.

> Dear Ben,
>
> Well, what can I say? You've certainly given me lots of material to talk about at dinner parties! Ben, even when you've been a complete pill and I've wanted to throttle you, I've still always cared about you. I think you are a really fantastic person and you have so much to give and offer. I have loved getting to know you and I think that there will be a definite emptiness in my class. (It will also be quiet!)
>
> Some of my fondest memories of this year have involved you—your fantastic poem on the Vietnam War; talking to you while you were in sick bay; sitting on the step of the staff house talking about having your operation on your legs, etc.—all these things!
>
> I hope that you can look back on your time here with

happiness. I am certain that you could be a success at whatever you put your mind to. Aim high, Ben, and don't sell yourself short. Be good!

Best wishes for a happy future!

Mark Stracey

When I was younger I read this letter to pick me up. I also read the letter when I was being lazy at school and in life generally. I love the last lines: "I am certain that you could be a success at whatever you put your mind to. Aim high, Ben, and don't sell yourself short!" I just hope that I haven't sold myself short in life, because I wouldn't like to let such a great person and friend down after everything he has done for me!

Thanks, from your good friend Ben Polis.

Fifth Year: Coeducational School, Time to Shape Up or Ship Out!

Fifth year was a real turning point in my life. My parents thought it would be beneficial if I went to a school in a new area. They thought that my reputation as a troublemaker would not follow me. This gave me the opportunity to put my future in my own hands. It was up to me now. I didn't have anyone else to blame if I didn't succeed according to my abilities, which my previous teachers believed I had not used fully. My new school was coeducational and Catholic.

My parents were a bit apprehensive about sending me to a coeducational school, believing that I would not be able to succeed with the distraction of females in my class. They felt I had done well at an all-boys school. However, this did not matter as much as my parents had anticipated. The reason for this was that when I was at an all-boys school, it was expected that we would act like jerks and fool around. Going to an all-boys school is like going to school with your football team. All-boys schools allow a lot more leeway with boisterous behavior. I learned pretty quickly that a coeducational school has a totally different environment. At a coeducational school you can't act like a jerk because you make yourself look like a fool in front of the girls. This would not have been the case if I had attended a coeducational school in my younger years. People believe that you grow out of ADD/ADHD, but that is not true. You just learn to control your behavior better as you mature. In theory, this should have been the case for me, but it was not. I still acted like the class clown because that's who I am. I will never change and I don't think I should have to change. If people don't like me, I believe that's their problem.

When I first started at my new school, it was not a big change. I made some friends pretty fast and I settled in pretty well. I still acted like a fool, but the difference this time was that I wanted to succeed at my schoolwork. I remember the first time I handed in an assignment. The teacher would not accept it. She didn't believe I had done it myself. At first, I was really angry, but I now understand why. I did no work in class; I called out constantly and didn't take any books to class. This was how I have always studied at school—by just listening to the teacher. I don't have the concentration to write things down, and, if I do, I get bored and blank out. Well, I handed in a perfect piece of work and got an A. But my father had to write a letter to say I had done it. It was during fifth year that I really started to use my self-help techniques. I guess I had always sort of used them, but I had not used them enough to understand their true power.

Well, I passed fifth year with average grades. I did fail two subjects—accounting and physical education—which seems pretty stupid considering that I should have excelled in those subjects. But again those subjects did not stimulate my interest and I deliberately failed them. You may be thinking, why would I deliberately fail? The reason was that I had completed three extra units in fourth year doing two fifth year subjects. So my theory was that it didn't matter if I failed two subjects. This sounds dumb, but this did let me pass my other subjects, which I was in danger of failing anyway. My parents were furious with my decision. My answer to this was: "It will be fine, it always is!" This became a bit of a catchphrase of mine when my parents were worried about my future. Again I was right and it was fine.

I did get suspended a couple of times in fifth year and had a number of after-school and Saturday detentions. These disciplinary actions were fueled by my disruptive behavior in class. But I was not fighting anymore like I had before. I also found that my disruptive behavior in classes got worse as I got older. There is a very good reason for this.

Below is my fifth year report card:

Comments from Homeroom Teacher: Ben has settled well into the fifth year homeroom and the calm and respectful atmosphere that we have developed. He is to be congratulated on his involvement in the cocurricular activities and for his cooperation in carrying out homeroom duties, including raffle ticket sales for fifth year social services causes. Ben is always courteous and well mannered. I look forward to witnessing and encouraging his continued academic development over the all-important second term. Thanks for your support in homeroom, Ben. A very successful term.

As you can see, my academic performance had improved considerably. But if I continued to get bad grades I would not get into college. So once again I had to improve or I was going to be labeled a loser. My first hurdle was to pass sixth year, which was no mean feat in itself. Well, the big year had arrived and it was sink or swim for me.

Sixth Year:
Who Would Have Thought
I Would Have Made It This Far?

During sixth year I made some very radical changes in my life, which I have stuck to ever since. These changes, in both thinking and implementation, I believe to be the determining factors in redirecting my life. I also feel they are an invaluable tool for your own child's schooling. I just wish I had discovered them earlier because my life would have been a lot easier.

Sixth year started and I had a point to prove to the world. I remember telling Mum, "I am going to show all those people who thought I was a loser!" I also remember writing down my goals at the start of sixth year:

Pass sixth year without getting kicked out!
Get an ENTER score over 60 (an ENTER score is the grade you get at the end of sixth year. It is out of a possible 99).

Get into college!

Pass college!

Make a million dollars before I am twenty-five!

Background on VCE Procedures

VCE (Victorian Certificate of Education) is awarded in Australia to sixth year students who pass four nominated sixth year subjects.

These subjects are measured by three assignments during the year. Called CATS, or common assessment tasks, these assignments are around two thousand words each and take forever! You do one CAT in each term, or half year. Along with this you do a number of minor work tasks that are not graded but you must pass them to get the VCE. This is followed by an exam at the end of the year. The workload in sixth year is the hard thing about getting your VCE. So this requires excellent organizational skills, which ADD/ADHD kids lack. But I was determined to be organized!

Term One. Freak to Geek in Three Months

I was a new person. My parents could not believe their eyes. I was doing homework but not a little homework. I had become the "Homework Machine"—this was what I called myself. The experts say that routine is vital for an ADD/ADHD child and even an adult, and they are bloody right! Let me tell you my daily routine during sixth year.

Go to school and try to act cool. At school I was still Ben Polis. I still got kicked out of classes. I disrupted classes, walked out of classes, and didn't go to classes. I don't know how many times during sixth year people asked me, "Are you passing?" "Yeah, of course!" I replied with a cheeky grin.

Go to after-school detention, get another detention for talking during my detention. Then do it all over again tomorrow.

Get the train home, give grief to train passengers, buy two potato cakes from the fish-and-chip shop and walk home.

Watch television for about an hour. Turn television off at five o'clock.

Take two Ritalin.

Go down to my room. Then clean my room and my desk.

Get a drink and some food to munch while doing homework, so I don't use the excuse of being hungry to stop doing homework.

Lock my door, turn on my stereo so I won't get bored.

By doing this I had created the perfect working environment for any student, but more important I had created the perfect working environment for an ADD/ADHD student.

Then I did the most amazing thing I have ever done in my life—I did homework and lots of it.

I started doing homework at five o'clock and then stopped at around eight to have dinner. But this is the most important thing that your child can learn from my routine. Once I had finished my dinner I *ran* back to my room and locked my door. Strange? Yes! But there is a very good reason for this. I ran to my room so I could not be distracted by anything else and prevented from doing my homework!

After dinner I studied till two in the morning—an incredible feat for any student but a miracle for someone with ADHD. The amazing thing about this whole picture I am painting for you is that my medication had worn off by this time of the night. But I had captured my limited concentration and directed it to my schoolwork. I can do this only if I take away all distractions.

Then I went to sleep and did it all over again the next day.

I did do a lot of homework in sixth year, but that was because I had to. Remember, I never did any work at school because I couldn't concentrate. I discovered a funny thing about all my sixth year teachers that year. I was always being lectured to settle down at school and do more schoolwork. But this all changed when I handed in my first-round CATS in term one.

I remember the day like it was yesterday. It was judgment day for me. I had not gone to school on that day, and my mother had driven me to get my grades. I walked into school and I remember being so nervous. I received my grades from the sixth year office and ripped the envelope open. All the other sixth year students were doing the same. I yelled out at the top of my lungs, *"I got four As and one B+!"* Highlighting my impulsivity again, this was followed by loud laughter. I replied to this, "Nah, seriously, I got straight As!" Then people started to grab the piece of paper from me to look at my grades. Then they were even checking the name to see if it was mine. I then ran like a bat out of hell to show my mum. She didn't believe me either. What the hell is wrong with all these people? I couldn't believe how many people thought I was *dumb*!

The most important thing I learned from my first-round CAT marks was that I had always thought and believed I could achieve at school, but I had never, ever proved it to myself. But now I had. I learned that if I applied myself I could achieve results far beyond my wildest dreams. I always believed that if you do something well and to your best ability, you can achieve. However, I had never put this into practice. I always did things to the bare minimum to just pass. I now live by the belief that if I am going to do something it must be to the best of my abilities. If it is not, I do not bother completing it. Along with this I also believe that if you get knocked down and don't succeed, you must try harder next time. As the saying goes, "Try, try, try again and you will succeed!"

My belief was tested by my father late one night. I was doing homework well past two o'clock. My father came into my room and asked me how it was going at school. I replied, "Everything is fine but I am sick of doing homework and I am tired and I want to go to bed." To my very upsetting surprise he told me that I was not doing enough homework and I wasted my time too much. He then told me that if I had tried harder I would have gotten straight As and that the one B+ I got would have been an A. This made me upset and angry. I told him to f*@# off and stop being so hard on me! I then told him that if it had been Adelaide, my sister, he would be the one doing her homework and she would be at the pub. My mother came downstairs when she heard the yelling. She told him that he expected too much from me.

I was so upset because I wanted my parents to be proud of me and tell me they were proud of me. I knew they were proud of me, but I could not believe what my father had told me. Looking back on it now, I understand what my father was really trying to get across. It wasn't that I had not tried enough or that I was lazy. He just wanted me to do well and the only way he has ever known to do well and get ahead in life is to work harder than everyone else. So what he was saying was, "Ben, you must try harder and harder so you will succeed." That's basically what I believe today. If I had tried harder I would have gotten straight As. I had reached my mental and physical boundaries and instead of stopping there, I should have pushed my boundaries until either they broke or I did. Sounds extreme, but that's what I believe!

Term Two. The Final Hurdle

Looking back on term two now, it makes me quite angry—not at the teachers or my parents or life in general. I get angry at myself. I had done really well in the first term, but I did not achieve the same results in the second. They were not bad—they were quite good—but they could have been better and they should have been. I sort of lost my way during term two. I still did all my homework, but it was not at the same high standard as previously. I had had enough of school and I wanted to finish.

I did not put the same amount of effort into my CATS. Once I had achieved a level I believed would get me a good grade, it was good enough. I had sinned against my own religion. I had not exceeded my boundaries—I had reached them and quit.

There were several reasons. The first is I really started to hate school and I didn't want to go anymore. I just wanted to sit at home and do my work there. But this was not possible. Or was it? The second reason was that I was sick of doing meaningless schoolwork that took up so much time and that I didn't learn anything from. I wanted to be at college now and learn about things I was interested in. I wanted to study business and the finer details of the economy. The third reason I hated being at school was the pure boredom. I hated all my subjects except economics. The work was mind-numbing rubbish.

So, as in previous years, I resorted to disruptive behavior to relieve the boredom. I disrupted most of my classes by calling out and just being stupid. People kept asking me, "How can someone so smart be such a *fool*?" I told them how it is: I just like to muck around!

This question of my intelligence would again be highlighted by one of my teachers when we had to start making decisions for college courses. I had my heart set on studying at Deakin College, doing a bachelor of business in commerce. I organized a meeting with her and told her what I wanted to study. She told me that people like me didn't go to college. She thought it would be better if I did a TAFE (Technical and Further Education) course. People usually go to TAFE if they don't make the grades for college. She thought that if I completed TAFE, I could apply for college later. This made me so angry. I told her that I wanted to go to college and I was going to get into a good one. She then asked me in a very sarcastic tone what my grades were for first term. I told her, in the same sarcastic tone she had used, and her whole mood changed. I then decided I had gotten this far without anyone else's help, so I was going to choose a college myself—and that's what I did.

My continuing disruptive behavior was not tolerated. I was constantly suspended and threatened with expulsion. I had made it so far, but I was now on the verge of being thrown out. The coordinator had developed a plan, which would hopefully see me through the rest of the year. When I felt, or the teacher felt, that I was going to lose it, I was to leave the classroom and go to the library. I loved this plan. It allowed me to self-medicate with self-imposed isolation as I did at home. The only problem was the library now had to contend with my behavior. Libraries and a disruptive ADHD student don't really work well, as you can imagine.

I got through the final term, but it was not an easy journey. I was expelled but not for as long as it could have been. The final exams were looming in around six weeks. By this time I hated school even more than previously. I wanted out, and I could not control my impulsive urges. I called out more and more and disrupted every class, including economics. This was not tolerated by the school. The problem was it was the most important part of the year. All the students were cramming hard and really trying to study. But I had reached my limits and could not concentrate or be bothered to study. The school had had enough and told me that I was not to come back to school. They said I was constantly disrupting exam preparations. However, I was to come to school every couple of days and hand in work and receive assignments to do. Along with this, I was allowed to sit my exams at the school instead of doing them in the city. So I guess I was really lucky that I was allowed to take my exams and was not expelled from them too. On a brighter note, this was just what I had wanted all along. This was perfect for me. It allowed me to finish my assignments in time, which would have been harder if I had stayed at school.

Looking back on this now, I wish I had stuck it out and controlled my erratic behavior a little better. By being at home I put myself at a disadvantage because I did not get the same level of exam preparation as everyone else. I did have the time to study at home. But I was not in a mental state to put in the hours required to pass the exams with flying colors. I had done enough work during the year to pass the exams well. But the marks I achieved in the second round of CATS and the exams underscored the predicament I had put myself in and its consequences.

I still did quite well considering I was not at school for the exam preparation. Most students would be pleased with results like mine. But I had sold myself short and I know that now. I had done no study to achieve two B+s and three Bs in my exams, so who knows what I could have achieved if I had applied myself better. But it does not matter—I still made it to college!

So I finally had done it. I passed sixth year and received my VCE. It only took six schools, five thousand detentions, three hundred days of suspension and a case of Ritalin. Passing sixth year is one of my proudest moments. I had finally proven all the doubters wrong. I would love to go back to my first year coordinator and wave my certificate in her face. Teachers like her do nothing for an ADD/ADHD student. Encouragement is the only way to get through to an ADD/ADHD student. It makes no sense constantly putting an ADD/ADHD student down because he will only start to believe what he is being told—that he is a troublesome burden to the school.

However, on a funny note, in sixth year there were some memorable moments that make me laugh. The first was putting the sixth year school captain in a wheeled trash can and shutting the lid, then wheeling her around the school. It was good for a laugh even though it was at her expense.

The second incident is one I will always be remembered for. It was the last day of school and I was allowed to attend. The last day of school is known as change of ID day. Everyone dresses up as someone else. For months, I had been thinking of who I would be. Then, like a lightning bolt, it hit me one day while I was getting yelled at by the director of students. I didn't like this man, and I wanted to make him look stupid but just didn't know how.

On the last day of school, he told me before we all got changed that I had better be on my best behavior. I told him I would and that I had a little surprise for him. He didn't have a clue what I had been concocting for months. I got changed and walked outside as though nothing was different.

I then started to order students around. I couldn't believe it— I had made such a great uniform to look like this teacher that people thought I was him. When everyone finally worked out it was me, they were in hysterics. When this teacher came to say good-bye to the sixth year, he was greeted with more hysterical laughter because I was imitating him behind his back. I walked up behind him and told him in his voice, "Tuck that shirt in or I will give you a detention, Ben Polis!" This was again followed by laughter. We had a photo taken together and I said, "How do you like your surprise?" He walked off and didn't come back. I had finally gotten the last laugh! It took only two years! This is definitely the best way to get back at a teacher you don't like. It provides years of payback when your classmates look at their yearbooks. So the moral to this story is, do not mess with a creative ADHD child because you will come off second best.

High School Hints

What parents must realize is that their child is not a baby anymore and is becoming a young adult. So he must be treated as one. Helping their child develop a structured environment is the most important thing parents can do. Along with helping their teenager be independent, parents must still show interest in their son. They must constantly check up on him to make sure he is not falling behind in school. However, this must not become annoying for your son, because then you risk pushing him away.

Lots of positive reinforcement is valuable at this stage of your son's life. Teens are very self-aware. It's all about who you are and who you are not. If you constantly find yourself telling your son off, you may be doing more damage than good. It's all about finding a happy medium.

Drugs will most probably come into play sometime in your son's life. However, a lot of ADD/ADHD teenagers get hooked on drugs because they use them to escape reality. And reality is often not a happy place! Therefore, make sure you monitor your son's life and look for warning signs. They are there, but many parents have no idea because they are caught up in their own world.

Challenges will come and go in your son's life, but at this age they often seem too big to handle alone. Just make sure your son understands that you are there for him and not just another problem for him. Talk to him and ask him how his day went, build a friendly relationship. In that way you can better understand and connect with your son.

One question that I'm often asked is: coed or all-boys school?

My preference is an all-boys school, but that's because I was very boisterous. I think it depends on so many factors that I can't say which one I recommend. It all depends on the individual. But let me say one thing: It's a lot easier to concentrate on math when you don't have a sixteen-year-old girl in front of you.

So remember: Support and understanding are crucial!

Ben Polis Is Going to the University! Yeah, Right!

I did not get into Deakin College because I forgot to change my course preferences. This again highlights my lack of organizational skills. Realizing that I'd forgotten to do this was one of the most upsetting moments in my life. Now it was in the lap of the gods. The placements came out and I couldn't believe it. I got into a better business college than I had ever imagined. I scored a TER (tertiary entry score) of 78.05 out of a possible 99.5, which is a good score. This again proved my ability when I had written down that I wanted an ENTER above 60 in my goals at the start of sixth year. The problem was that to take most business courses I needed something above 81, which I did not get. It was such a worrying time in my life because I knew that if I had tried as hard as I had in the first term, I would have got around an 85 and easily gotten into any course. But again luck was on my side. I was accepted into the School of Business at Royal Melbourne Institute of Technology (RMIT) in the undergraduate bachelor of business in administration program. I was the last person to be let into the course and I had the lowest TER. I couldn't believe it. I have always felt that I have been lucky and that someone is looking out for me. I don't know who it is, but thanks, whoever you are!

So I had finally achieved my personal goal. I was going to college, and I had managed all this with a learning disability. I would like to know what that learning disability is because I haven't worked it out yet. I have often wondered what my life would be like if I didn't have ADHD, and I don't think I would be as successful as I am today. I like to think of myself as one of the lucky people to have ADHD, because I feel that I wouldn't be as intelligent if I didn't have ADHD.

The greatest thing for me about college is not the actual study. The thing I love the most is when I see people on the train who I went to high school with and they ask me where I am going. I love the reaction I get when I tell them I am going to college. I always had such a motivational problem when I had to go to school, but when I get up for college I wake up with a smile on my face. Every day I go to college is a reminder of how far I have come. I am damn proud that I am at college, and I can't wait for the graduation day when my name is called and I receive my degree. I have pictured this day over and over again in my head and it gets better every time.

College Is the Place to Be If You Have ADHD

College is definitely the place for me. My fourth year English teacher told me one day that I would be more suited to college than high school. I never really understood this until I got there.

The reason college is so good for an ADD/ADHD student is because of the learning style that they use.

The first thing I realized when I went to college was that acting like a fool is not tolerated. It is not that they don't allow it. It is that you have chosen to be there, and if you act like a fool what the hell are you doing there? You are there because you want to be there and you want to do well, not for your parents but for yourself. If you do not apply yourself to your highest abilities, the only person you are letting down is yourself.

The second reason college is the place for an ADD/ADHD student is that in college you sit in a lecture for a couple of hours and use all your concentration on listening. Then you have a break for an hour or two, which lets you replenish your concentration stores, and then you have a tutorial for about an hour. Then you go home and study in your own learning style. This is not possible in high school because you are locked up for hours on end with many distractions. But in college, if you feel that you cannot concentrate and you need a break before the next class, you can just walk out anytime. In high school if you walked out of a class you received a detention.

The third reason college is the place to be if you have ADD/ADHD is that you choose the courses you take. We all know that ADD/ADHD people have interests and often hyperfocus on these topics. So if you choose a course that you are interested in, you can direct this focus on your course and achieve tremendously. But the key to this success is to choose a course that you are truly interested in. I know if I had chosen to study accounting only because accountants are paid well, I would have failed at it. I cannot concentrate on things that I am not interested in. So instead of using this as a disadvantage, you should, as I have, turn it around and use it as an advantage.

There is one thing you must be very careful of when your child goes to college. The ordered routine of high school does not exist at college. You do not have to go to class or even hand in work. You do not have a teacher yelling at you to turn in an assignment—it is all up to you. Along with this, when you first go to college you are not told anything—you have to work out everything yourself. This is a recipe for disaster for an ADD/ADHD student. To counter this problem, I advise that you or your child find out as much as possible about the college beforehand. Find out where your course office is and where you will hand in your assignments. Also, keep a diary of all due dates and be extremely organized. I advise that you get the phone numbers of all your lecturers before you start the course. This will allow you to find out answers to questions concerning your courses when they arise. The most important thing an ADD/ADHD student should do before attending college is to locate the library. This may seem stupid, especially in my case since I hate libraries, but libraries can be an ADD/ADHD student's best friend. Libraries provide the perfect working environment for an ADD/ADHD student because they are quiet and the student can isolate himself, allowing him to capture his limited concentration. Also, it's a great place to find girls! Another service that college often provides is learning aids. You can receive extended time on your exams and even get scribes to write down notes.

I achieved good results in my first year at college and was happy with my choice of subjects. But while I was handing in an assignment I saw a poster for a new course. It was a bachelor of business in entrepreneurial studies and I was immediately interested. I found out a bit more about it and I applied. The degree was designed for students who had good business ideas or were already running their own businesses. I didn't have a business but I had lots of good ideas. I had an interview and I could feel it was not going well. So I decided that I would again use my ADHD as an advantage. I had already started writing this book but didn't want anyone to know. I told the interviewer what I was doing and how I was helping other kids who suffer from ADD/ADHD. She was pretty impressed and I knew that I had gotten in.

So that's what I am doing now, and I love it. It allows me to express all my weird and wacky ADHD ideas without narrow-minded people knocking them as they did in the past. I guess only time will tell if these ideas of mine will be successful. But I believe if I try hard enough and push myself I will succeed.

Well, that's my life. There are many things I am not proud of and some things I am extremely proud of. I hope that I have provided a more positive outlook on ADD/ADHD. I was a very upset and angry child. But now I could not be happier. I would not change a thing in my life because I feel that I have learned a lot from my experiences and that I can teach other people as a result of them. I remember one day only a couple of months ago at work when someone asked me, "What are you so happy about?"

I replied, "Life in general!"

Tips for College

I can't stress how important it is for parents not to determine what degree their son chooses. So many parents try to live their dreams through their children, and all it does is stuff up their child's life. Let him choose what he wants to do. If he wants to be a tree surgeon let him. By the time your son finally makes it to college—if he does at all—he will be an adult. However, he may still be mentally very immature. Therefore support from parents is still necessary. If he has moved away, make sure you stay in contact and make him feel like he is still a part of the family.

Being prepared is critical to college success. If you are organized, college should be easy. People often get into trouble with their college studies because they feel like they have more time than they really do. All it takes is needing a little longer than you expected with a few assignments or losing the disk containing your homework, and your college life can become a disaster. I have seen so many people in college who have trouble with a subject at the start of the year but try not to think about it until it's too late. Out of sight is not out of mind, when it comes to college degrees. You can't cram at the last minute! Get help at the start of the term if you are having a hard time in a class. Colleges have many helpful programs, but students seem not to ask for help until it's too late.

College Study Techniques

The most important thing I ever learned in college was this: Ps get degrees! Meaning if you pass, you get a degree, and that's what you go to college for. College can be very difficult for a lot of people. But I believe that when you study such a wide variety of subjects, you will find some that you are good at and others that you are really bad at. Appropriate studying techniques, however, will help make your life easier.

College classes include a lot of lectures, which are sometimes extremely boring, but that's life. ADD/ADHD students need to establish what type of learning style works best for them.

Most ADD/ADHD students are visual learners, which is good for attending lectures. Usually the most important and stressful thing about college is the end of the term exam. It's often this exam that determines if you pass or fail, so I think this has the most importance.

How do you determine what is going to be on the exam? During most of the term, you're taught a lot on one topic. But how do you determine what is and what is not worth remembering? You can take a calculated guess on what will be on the exam, but you must do so at the start of the course.

Colleges these days often put lecture notes on the Internet for you to download and print. It is a great idea because you don't have to sit and write frantically for hours information that you're not sure is important. You should print and bind the whole term's lecture notes in one go. This helps disorganized ADD/ADHD students a lot. Don't print them bit by bit every week because you will lose some or forget to download them.

The next thing is to ask your professors for old exams from the years past. Professors will often hand these out at the end of the course, but try to get them at the start. Read them over in the first few weeks of term, and that way you will get a better understanding of what will be on the exam. More important, you will listen more attentively when these topics are covered in lectures. Basically you will be remembering and therefore studying what is important.

Highlight and mark these topics of importance on the printed lecture notes, so you can refer to the significant stuff and jog your memory when it comes to exam preparation.

Establishing a good study group is great for ADD/ADHD

students because they often want to ask questions but are unable to during lectures. You will also find it easier to recall information that you have learned in a study group because you remember conversations about topics and other people's opinions a lot easier than what some boring lecturer has mumbled to two hundred students.

Remember, college is meant to be fun, so get your schoolwork done so you can hit the clubs!

My Life Today

The book you are reading was written when I was nineteen. I am now twenty-two, so a lot has changed. I'm a little older and a little fatter. But, boy, this book has taken me places that I never imagined.

After I wrote my book I had to get a publisher. I discovered that it is extremely hard to get a book published, especially in Australia. I submitted the book to a few publishers and I got nothing but rejection. But I was prepared for that. I hit Dad up for a loan and decided to self-publish my book. I was confident because I had already had books ordered from my website. So basically I printed some books, found a book distributor, and then got on the promotions trail.

The evening before the 2001 Australian Open I sent off my media releases to all the major television current affairs programs just to see what would happen. The next morning I went to watch my favorite tennis player, Lleyton Hewitt. And then I had the surprise of my life. At nine o'clock my mobile phone began ringing, as I sat at the match. All the media people were chasing me for my story. My phone didn't stop ringing, which was really annoying because the reporters were eating into my very valuable partying time.

I chose to talk to the major current affairs program. Two months later my story appeared, and I became an Australian bestselling author within twenty-four hours. The only problem was I had to print more books. I asked Dad for another loan. So after that I did all the major TV, radio, and print media interviews I could do in Australia. I did a national speaking tour of both Australia and New Zealand. Oh, yeah, I had to leave college because I was too busy.

But all this success did not make me happy. I wrote this book with the intention of cracking the American market. I tried for over a year to get some media exposure there. I got absolutely nothing. I sent off over one thousand media releases, which my mates helped me fold, from my bedroom in Australia. I didn't get one response. So I decided to come to America in February 2003 to see what I was doing wrong. Once I got here I realized that there are a lot more people trying to do what I was doing—that is, trying to sell something.

I came home with my tail between my legs. I was beaten; I had basically given up. I had been back home in Australia for three days sitting on my bed in a state of depression, when I decided to get up. I check my e-mails first thing in the morning every morning. I remember turning my computer on and thinking to myself: What is the point?

I sat down and started to read my e-mails. Then I let out an almighty scream! I had an e-mail from a reporter from *USA*

Today. You may have heard of it. Well, I hadn't. I then checked my media database and then let out another almighty scream. I read that it was the largest newspaper in America!

I spoke to the reporter and she said she had been reading my book for the past six months and she loved it! So the paper did a story on me and my life changed forever. The reporter wrote that I had self-published, and over the next forty-eight hours I was being contacted by the largest publishing companies in the world. Picture this: twenty-one-year-old kid sitting in his underwear in the middle of the night on the other side of the world speaking to publishers that he had only dreamed about. Well, that was me and it was very cool! They were asking me who my agent was because they wanted to discuss U.S. and world rights for my book. I said I would just get my mum. . . .

One month later I caught a plane from Melbourne, and twenty-one hours later I was in New York City to meet with all the major publishing houses. Let me tell you, if you thought I had trouble sitting still in class, it was nothing like being stuck in a tin can for twenty-one hours! Well, guess what? I sold the rights and the book you are reading is proof!

So I guess I finally made it!

Part Two

Strategies for Success

What Is It Really Like
to Have ADD/ADHD?

I feel that the strategies I will discuss in the following pages are the most fundamentally useful tools for overcoming and using ADD/ADHD to your advantage. Some elite doctors who treat ADD/ADHD will dispute this statement. They believe that medication is the only way to treat ADD/ADHD. I am not a critic of medication, because I used to take it nearly every day, but only when I needed it. (As an adult, the only time I have used Ritalin is when I wrote this book.)

The argument I put forward about medication is quite simple. Medication does not stop but only limits the impulsive urges to which ADD/ADHD children and even adults are prone. If your son is on medication and his brain tells him to jump from a tree, no medication is going to stop this thought process. Therefore, you must teach your son to think about the consequences of jumping from the tree. I use a deciphering technique to decide which is a good thought. I often try to put myself in other people's shoes. I ask myself: If I were someone else, would

I jump from the tree? This allows me to decide between a good thought and a bad thought. The argument I often get when I present this technique is that ADD/ADHD kids are too impulsive to think before they jump. This is often true. But if you drill this into your son every day, he will eventually remember it when he is doing something abnormal. People also say that ADD/ADHD kids don't think before they act. But I disagree. ADD/ADHD kids do think before they act, but they do not think about the consequences of their actions. As you know, every action has a reaction but ADD/ADHD kids often forget this.

Parents often ask why their child is so angry and violent. Some people think these are symptoms of ADD/ADHD. But this is not true. I have severe ADHD and I was an extremely angry and violent person. But as I grew up I had no reason to be angry and violent and bash innocent people and my family. Anger and violence are not *symptoms* of ADD/ADHD but *results* of ADD/ADHD. To understand why your child is so angry, upset, and violent you must understand the world he lives in. People who do not have ADD/ADHD don't really understand what it is like to have ADD/ADHD, and therefore they do not understand how to deal with it and control it. I will try to explain what it is like to have ADD/ADHD, so you can better understand your own child.

ADD/ADHD is often classified as a disorder that affects concentration, usually associated with naughty or just bad children. This is a common belief of people who do not understand ADD/ADHD, and the media subsequently reinforces this. ADD/ADHD children are often labeled as bad kids because of their erratic behavioral and social patterns. But ADD/ADHD goes much further than this. To understand this, you must look at it from your child's point of view.

Have you ever done something and afterward wondered, Why the hell did I do (or say) that? That is exactly what it is like to have ADD/ADHD. But the only problem is you don't understand why your brain told you to act that way.

Here is an example I often use: If a normal person's brain tells him, I am hungry so feed me, what does he do? He feeds himself by making a sandwich or something. This seems normal to you, because your brain told you that you were hungry.

Now let's look at it from an ADD/ADHD perspective. You are sitting down watching television and just relaxing. You have the same thought: I am hungry, so feed me. So what do you do? You get up to feed yourself. You are out of your seat and running to the kitchen. But as you are running to the kitchen you see the dog sitting on the carpet. Then your brain tells you to kick the dog just like your brain told you to make a sandwich. Then the dog bites you and you kick it again. The dog runs off and you wonder why the dog bit you. But then your brain tells you that you're still hungry so you go to make a sandwich. But just before you make a sandwich your mum yells at you for kicking the dog. But you're wondering why your mum is angry because you were just making a sandwich. Then you go mental and start to kick your mum and tell her that she is a *cow*. But you don't realize that you just called your mum a cow because you just wanted to make a sandwich. Then you go back and continue watching television.

Now look at it from a mother's perspective. How the tables turn! My son was running to the kitchen, kicked the dog, the dog bit my son, my son then kicked the dog again, and the dog ran off. So I yelled at my son for kicking the dog. Then my son hit me and called me a *cow*. Then he sat down and continued watching television as if nothing had happened.

The mother then starts to cry because she can't understand what is wrong with her son. She asks herself, Why did my son call me a *cow* and hit me? She then thinks to herself, Maybe I am just a bad mother. Then depression sets in and the mother just can't handle it anymore.

Here's another example of how your son's thought process works. You and your son are going shopping and a large woman walks past and bumps you with her stomach. You think to yourself, Watch what you're doing, fatty!

Now look at it from your son's perspective. You are going shopping with your mum, but you really hate shopping and want to be watching television. You are already in a bad mood because your mum won't take you to the toy shop. So you are walking along insulting your mum. You are so angry you are going to explode. Then a large woman walks past and bumps you with her stomach. You turn around and yell at the top of your lungs, "Stupid fat tub, watch where you wave that thing. You're so fat your stomach has its own zip code!" Then your mum yells at you because some fat lady knocked into you.

Looking at this from your mum's perspective, you are the one at fault. She is crying inside, asking herself, Why can't he just keep his mouth shut? Looking at it from your perspective, you think it's your mum's fault because if she had just taken you to the toy shop, none of this would have happened—and the fat tub deserved it.

What Makes an ADHD Child Angry and Violent?

We all know that ADHD children are often extremely violent, especially toward their family. Parents many times do not understand why their child acts violently toward the people he loves but at the same time manages not to vent this anger on other people. Some parents believe that they are the cause of their child's anger and that they must be at fault. To understand this and therefore correct the problem, parents must again take a snapshot of their child's life.

Normal children attend school with few obstacles. But an ADHD child is faced with huge obstacles every day. At such a young age these obstacles seem as huge as crossing the English Channel. To understand this concept I will again describe your child's world. I like to use an example of a volcano to describe ADHD anger. Anger builds up like lava in a volcano until it reaches such a point it explodes. But this is where parents often get confused. They do not understand why something as trivial as asking an ADHD child to brush his teeth can trigger an angry outburst. This is when the volcano example comes in. But the best thing about the volcano example is that, like volcanoes, you can gauge when and where your child is going to explode. You, too, can measure and predict when and where one of these outbursts is going to happen. But, unlike with volcanoes, you can also slowly release pressure so it does not build up and cause widespread destruction.

The Volcano

Your son wakes up in the morning tired after only a couple of hours' sleep. You think to yourself, How can he be so tired? I put him to bed early. Many people don't realize the difficulty that ADHD people have in getting to sleep. It's not that they are not tired—they are often exhausted after an energetic day. They just can't get to sleep because, unlike normal people whose minds stop when they go to bed, an ADHD person's mind never stops. Stimulant medication, such as Ritalin, also causes insomnia. So your son wakes up tired and has to face another day of obstacles. He wakes up in a bad mood and then has to go to school. The first layer of lava has flowed onto the volcano.

When he finally gets to school after many frantic minutes, he finds himself in a restricted environment. The class is told to open their books. But your son does not hear this command because he is not concentrating. Again, this is another false, common belief— that ADHD kids don't concentrate. Your son is not concentrating on the teacher but on something else that he finds more stimulating. His concentration has already been sapped from lack of sleep. He is then told off for not opening his book, but he can't understand why he is being told off because he doesn't remember being told to open his book. He is now getting even more confused, especially if he lacks academic skills. He sees the rest of the students doing work but he can't do it, and he doesn't understand why. The second layer of lava flows onto the volcano of anger.

It's time for lunch, but your son has to stay back, either to finish his work or for some misdemeanor. He looks at the other kids playing and thinks to himself, Why am I not playing outside?

However, now he is the only one in the classroom and he can finish his work because he has created the perfect working environment for himself. But he still can't understand why he couldn't do it before. He thinks to himself, Why am I so different from the other kids? The third layer of lava has been laid.

Lunch is over, but your son has had no chance to burn off any of his extra energy or frustration. He now has to go back to class and do more unstimulating schoolwork. He sees his friend next to him making a paper airplane. He thinks to himself, That seems more interesting than doing math, so he makes one, too. But he makes his airplane bigger and better than his friend's. ADHD kids just don't understand the concept of being subtle. Your son is now so interested in making his airplane that he is in a totally different world. This is referred to as hyperfocusing, to which ADHD people are prone. He now wants to test his plane, so he throws it across the classroom. It hits a girl in the head, and he is sent outside. While sitting outside he thinks to himself, Why does everyone pick on me so much? My friend was also making a paper airplane, but he didn't get in trouble.

This is where ADHD kids suffer the most. They don't really understand how distracting or over-the-top their behavior is because it seems so normal to them. The fourth layer of lava has now flowed onto the volcano of anger.

You pick up your son and he seems really happy. You believe he is happy because he had a good day at school. But really he is happy because he is out of school and safe with people who love him and don't treat him differently. Your son goes home and throws his bag on the floor right in the way of everyone. He sits down and watches television for hours and hours. You think he is just being lazy, but he is not.

It's now time to do homework. But you know and he knows that it is not going to happen without a fight. You turn the television off and you have now successfully triggered the volcano of anger. But you are thinking, What the hell did I do that was so bad? I just turned the television off. Your son then goes into a rage, yelling and swearing at you. But you're not at fault—you're just the lava field on which your son can release the anger built up in the course of the day.

There are a couple of things you must realize when your son explodes like this. The first is that when your son works himself up into these fits of anger, he does not know what he is doing. He is so angry that when he explodes, he does not understand what he is doing or saying. He may punch you and kick you, but he honestly does not know what he is doing. This seems really strange to normal people, but it is true. The thing about these outbursts is that they can last only a couple of minutes or maybe an hour. But afterward he can be as nice as pie and settled and calm.

Normal people will see this as a total disregard for their behavior. But what makes it even worse is that parents will punish their child after he has released his anger. Then the whole cycle starts again. Your son does not know why he has now been sent to his room because he can't even remember punching and kicking you—thus pouring the first layer of lava again.

People often ask me why it is the parents who receive the raw end of the violence. It's not that your son hates you. It is the exact opposite. He loves you and that's why he does it. It sounds strange but that's what happens. He knows that if he explodes like this, you will still love him. You are your child's lava field, and lava fields are used over and over again to release the pressure.

What to Do If You Have an Angry and Violent ADHD Child

Violence can destroy any family, but it makes it so much harder to handle when you love the violent person unconditionally. My parents once described me as an uncontrollable child, which is quite true. But what they didn't realize was that I couldn't control my own actions. So I guess they had no chance. It took me many years to understand why I was so angry and violent. But when I did, my whole life changed and so did my parents'. The thing about anger is it builds up until it explodes and then people you love get hurt. But there is an answer and a way to control anger, which I learned.

I have already outlined why ADHD kids are so angry but I haven't told you what you really want to know. How do I stop it?

The journey to anger reduction is long and hard, but when you reach the end of that journey it is worth every step. The first thing you must do is understand why your son is angry. It may seem that one incident caused the violent explosion. But you must look beyond that and see into your son's world. His social environment is often the cause of most of his anger. The answer is to change it. The only way to do so is to build up your son's confidence so he believes he can take on the world. Most people don't know what it is like to be constantly put down every day for things that they think are normal, to be told that they're bad kids and just plain dumb.

Building self-confidence can be done in only two ways. The first is through academic performance. But the problem arises: How can you teach an ADHD kid who doesn't want to learn? This is a question I often get from parents. They say it sounds good in theory but the implementation is nearly impossible. I totally agree with this, but there is an answer. The problem is that ADHD kids learn differently from normal kids. Using the learning system employed by schools is like trying to teach your child in another language.

The second way is to build confidence by sports or drama. We all know that ADHD kids are very energetic. They often excel at sports but they have little confidence in themselves. The other problem is that sports are often team sports and ADHD kids have trouble with social interaction. If sports and schoolwork are not implemented properly they can be counter-productive.

When using sports to build confidence I suggest individual sports. This allows your son to develop a sense of responsibility for his actions. It also creates a sense of personal achievement lacking in team sports. How many coaches do you think are going to like a low-concentration threshold player when trying to give orders or plays? I know—not many. Even if your son is not good at his individual sport, I suggest that you speak to his coach. If he never wins, who really cares? It's all about building confidence. You should tell the coach of your son's condition and then tell the coach how to help. Even giving your son an encouragement award can be extremely beneficial.

Once you have built your son's confidence up it's time to mold him into a more settled person. I have already told you that your son cannot be responsible for his actions because he does not understand what he is doing wrong. I bet that you have yelled at your son over and over again and it seems as though he is not listening. Well, you are right. You can yell at an ADHD child for hours and hours and he won't hear you because ADHD people have this uncanny knack of shutting the outside world off from themselves. *To get through to an ADHD child, throw all normal disciplinary actions out the window.*

To really reduce anger, you must show your son what he is doing wrong when he is doing it. ADHD children are very visual and experience most things through their eyes. To get through to an ADHD child you must show him exactly what he is doing *at the time*. Not afterward, not even ten minutes later. As soon as he does something you must show him what he is doing or he will forget and the whole disciplinary action is useless.

A video camera and a tape recorder can be a parent's best friends. If your child is throwing a temper tantrum I suggest that you record it and play it back to him as soon as possible. Lock the child in a room and make him watch it over and over again until he realizes what he has said or done. But don't let him out of his room until he has told you exactly what he has done wrong. This can be a life-changing moment for an ADHD child because he finally sees what he is doing wrong. The greatest thing about this tactic is that the next time your child goes crazy, all you need to do is get out the video camera. This visual cue tells him that he is acting as he did the last time he was recorded on video.

When your son has calmed down, I suggest that you sit him down and make him a sandwich and a drink and tell him that you love him. Your son is acting like this because his world is so hard to live in. He feels isolated, different, and unloved. By showing him that you care for him instead of yelling at him and reinforcing his self-doubt, you are making him feel better about himself.

I also suggest that when your son does go mental you should let him go. Don't stop him or try to restrain him unless he is breaking things or endangering himself or other people. Your son has to release his volcano of anger, and if he doesn't, it will only build up more and more.

You can also try to predict when and where one of these violent outbursts is going to happen. Certain things trigger these outbursts. I have learned that when I do not let off steam, I often take out my frustrations on other people. By recording the dates, times, and the circumstances of the outbursts you can better predict future ones. If a pattern emerges, you can counter this by deliberately releasing your child's anger in short bursts, for example, playing catch, kicking a football, and so on.

The secret to releasing the volcano is to learn to live with it and not to restrain it. Your son must release his anger in short controlled bursts. One of the boys I tutor is quite violent at school, like I was. One day when I was trying to tutor him, I was getting nowhere. I could see he was angry and just wanted to explode. So I decided that if he was going to explode, the best person to vent his anger at would be me. I took him outside and we had the biggest fight—it lasted about forty minutes. His mother came outside and could not believe her eyes. Her son was kicking me, biting me, punching me, and pulling my hair. His eyes were lit up and he looked mad. Most people would have been scared, but I knew exactly what he was going through. It wasn't that he hated me, because I know he loves me dearly, it was just that he had to release his anger. It's pretty hard to explain this to parents because it seems so wrong. It's like I am encouraging him to be violent. But what I was doing was allowing him to release his anger on me so that he would not release it at school, where he gets into trouble.

The only problem is it teaches him that violence solves things. So, afterward, I lay next to him on the ground and we looked up at the sky for about fifteen minutes. I then explained to him that he couldn't act like this toward other people because they don't understand how much fun it is. After this, we did his homework. We had never had such a productive day of homework. This was due to him freeing his mind of anger and hate for the world, and especially schoolwork.

Another problem is that I don't know how many mothers like to have their hair pulled. None, I suspect. I then thought about this a little more. Then it hit me. Martial arts do three great things for ADHD kids. The first is that it allows them to release their anger in a controlled environment. The second is that it teaches them to understand when and where they can use their fighting skills. Hopefully not on their sisters. The third is that it creates further self-esteem because they receive colored belts for their achievements.

The last thing I would like to mention about anger is that you must address it with an open mind. Sometimes you must condemn it and sometimes you have to encourage it. Controlled anger gives your child an outlet when he feels as if he is going to explode. My mum often says, "Go for a run on the beach and let your agro out." It works!

To Medicate or Not to Medicate? That Is the Question

The issue of medication is one of the hottest topics in the ADD/ADHD network. Parents are often extremely confused and concerned about the side effects of stimulant medication. Most parents and the media have no idea how it works or what it does. When I was younger I had some concerns about using Ritalin. Back then, I blamed it for my lack of height. I am only 165 centimeters tall (five feet six inches) and I haven't grown since I was about fourteen. I laugh at this now because, in fact, I am taller than both my parents, so I have come to the conclusion that it was not the medication but just genetics.

It makes me extremely angry when I hear in the media and from some doctors that medication is wrong and that we are breeding a generation of addicted children. The first thing parents must understand is that it is basically impossible to become addicted to this medication. This is where I feel the bad press about this medication comes from.

So How Do ADD Drugs Work, in English?

The brain works by sending electric impulses through brain cells. In a "normal" brain these impulses are sent and received undisturbed. In an ADD/ADHD brain these impulses are interrupted, so the next cell does not receive the whole message. The medication basically increases these impulses so more messages are sent. It also limits the natural enzyme that destroys these messages.

Here's another way of looking at it. Imagine the brain as a computer network sending e-mail messages. In the ADD/ADHD brain, when an e-mail is sent only a quarter of the e-mail is received by the next computer. The network cable is faulty because one of the wires is not connected properly. The medication sends more e-mails so that the whole e-mail is understood. It also reconnects the faulty network wire, allowing the whole e-mail to be sent to the next computer.

Well, if you understood that, you are a whole lot smarter than I am because it took me a long time to grasp this concept. This is the reason I am writing this book—I am sick and tired of trying to understand all this medical mumbo jumbo in ADD/ADHD books. The books continually say, "We believe this" or "It is understood." As best as I can work out, lots of doctors have lots of ideas on how they think ADD/ADHD works. But no one knows for sure.

Side Effects of Stimulant Medication

If anyone ever tells you that there are no side effects of stimulant medication, they are wrong. There are many, but how much they are felt and what types they are are different for every person. If you are wondering whether to use this medication you must first of all weigh the pros and cons. If the side effects are very bad, then of course you should not use the drug. But don't just dismiss it right away. There are a number of medications on the market and you should try all of them if necessary.

The known side effects of these drugs are only short-term. There are no known long-term side effects. Short-term side effects are felt both during and after the medication has gone through your system. The longest-lasting side effect is insomnia. This is a real issue with this medication, often missed because parents are not sleeping in the same room as their child. Many children have trouble falling asleep when taking these drugs. It basically feels like you have drunk a lot of coffee during the day. Then when you try to fall asleep because you are physically tired, your mind just can't turn off.

But I believe that the side effects do not outweigh the benefits of these drugs. I also believe that without these drugs I would not have succeeded as I have. Without these drugs I would not have graduated from high school and most likely would have ended up in a juvenile detention center. And I wouldn't have been able to start writing this book, let alone finish it.

Here are other possible side effects:

appetite loss
fullness in the stomach
fatigue
headaches
dizziness
blurred vision

depression
irritability
increased tension
tearfulness

Only a couple of these side effects may be experienced by your child and usually just for a couple of months, until your child's body adjusts to the medication.

The danger of using medication is that parents feel that it is the answer to all their problems. Well, let me tell you, it is not. It only helps. Some people believe that medication will work straight away. This is not true. It takes months and months and even years. Remember my behavioral pattern in seventh grade? I was on medication and I was still the same old Ben. Within twelve months my behavior had changed drastically. I was a new kid; I had started to understand the way my brain works. When I was on medication I started to understand how I was meant to behave. I also deliberately changed the way I thought. I tried to pay attention at school and I tried to behave. It was not the medication, it was the better understanding of how my brain works. But then in third year I was still on medication and I chose to revert to my old ways. No medication will change your child overnight—it is a lifelong journey of learning to deal with ADD/ADHD and how to control it.

The Question of Medication

Some doctors believe that people like me should be medicated around the clock. I was at a conference in Sydney when a doctor made this ridiculous statement. It made me so angry. I feel this belief comes from our quick-fix society. Today, when someone has a cold he goes to the doctor and wants a pill to fix it. Well, ADD/ADHD can't be fixed with a pill. If someone out there does have a pill for this, please let me know! It would be most appreciated!

The first thing you must understand is that although medication is the best way to treat ADD/ADHD, it does not solve it. I have heard of a mother medicating her son all day and then giving him a sleeping pill when he got home from school so she would not have to deal with him. I would like to meet this mother and ask her when is her son going to learn to deal with and understand his ADD/ADHD if he is knocked out like a zombie all day and night? This is my argument against these powerful drugs. I am pro-medication—but only when you need it. Do you take headache tablets when you don't have a headache? No, of course you don't. So why do parents give their children these powerful drugs when the children are behaving well? If you do this, your son will never learn to deal with his ADD/ADHD. Do you think when he turns eighteen and moves out and stops taking his medication, he is suddenly going to be able to control his erratic behavior?

I strongly believe that the only way to resolve ADD/ADHD is to learn to deal with it. I know that is why I have done so well—not because I take Ritalin, but because I learned to understand and develop practical strategies so I could function properly in society. I suggest that you medicate your child only when he needs it, usually at school and social functions. If your child is young, I can understand medicating him often. But as your child gets older he must learn to understand how to control his actions. People often think you grow out of ADD/ADHD, but this is not true. You just learn to control it better.

The Problems with Overmedication

Be careful about overmedicating. The thing about taking so much medication both in high dosages and over weeks without breaks is it makes your life a living hell. If you give your son too much medication it puts him into a zombie state. I hate this state and it makes me feel paranoid. I have often taken too much medication when doing homework and it's pretty scary. You go into a state of zombieness. I often find myself staring into thin air, concentrating on nothing. To do the simplest tasks seems impossible. I also find myself twitching and picking at my skin and I can't stop.

The problem with taking too much medication over a long period is that it drains your brain. You have to remember that this medication makes you hyperfocus on things. So if you take it for weeks without breaks, it is like extreme concentration for hours on end. It's like overworking yourself when you're not doing anything. I have found that when I take medication for long periods of time, it creates the worst insomnia. I can be as drunk as a skunk and I just can't fall asleep. Along with this, it produces the worst headaches. I call these "Ritalin headaches." These are often felt a couple of hours after the medication has worn off. They can be treated with a simple headache tablet.

When to Medicate

I believe the only time you should medicate your child is when he needs it. At school it is often essential. I don't have a problem with this because I took medication all the time at school. Other times it is needed are when starting homework, at family functions, while working, at social events, and when playing sports. But I believe it should never be taken on weekends unless really needed. Also, it should not be taken during school breaks. It's all about medication in moderation.

You must give your son time to recover after the school week. It is not a proven fact, but medication might cause reduced growth due to reduced appetite. However, there may also be other causes that we don't know yet. So it is very important to give your son plenty of breaks from medication to allow him to eat and grow.

I believe taking too much medication over a long period of time also produces counterproductive results. If your son takes too much medication, it drains him physically and especially mentally. When he is coming down off the medication he is mentally exhausted. The slightest thing may trigger a violent or erratic outburst.

Many people will dispute these statements. My argument is simply that we all know what it feels like when you work too hard. For example, if you do too many hours of overtime at work within a few months you will be physically and mentally exhausted. The slightest thing will annoy you. Well, that's exactly what it feels like when you take these medications for long periods of time. Your brain is in a hyper state for hours a day. But your child is not doing anything. He may be playing with friends and his mind is racing at a million miles an hour. So I believe that taking medication for long periods without breaks can actually aid bad behavior, because the child is mentally exhausted and is only propped up by more medication. Therefore he is more prone to losing it when frustrated as a result of being mentally and physically exhausted. I just ask that parents keep this in mind.

You should never give your son medication when he is doing nothing. It may make your life easier but it is cruel. When your son is on medication his brain is overstimulated and is in hyper mode. He is thinking frantically and must be stimulated either by physical or mental means. If your son is on medication you must give him things to do. If he is just sitting in front of the television he is hyperfocusing on a box. Ever wonder why your son is twitching and so fidgety when he is on medication? It is because he is mentally unstimulated and it's also a side effect of the drug. By rubbing and picking his skin he is hyperfocusing on that. Not a very nice experience, I can tell you.

How Should Medication Be Taken?

Your child should take his medication himself. It is all right for you to hand it to him, but he must learn to take it himself. It should be taken with food because this releases it more slowly. If I take it without food it hits me like a hammer and I go straight into a zombie state. In my experience, it takes about forty minutes to feel any effects. Around an hour and a half after medication has been taken, the greatest effects are felt. You should tell your child why he is taking the pill and how it improves his behavior, concentration, and so on. I suggest filming him when he is on medication and when he is not. This will help him understand the appropriate ways to act. And when he is not acting appropriately he will learn to self-medicate, which is extremely important as he gets older.

The biggest challenge for your son is taking medicine at school. My dosage was two tablets in the morning and two tablets at lunch. My mother put my tablets in my lunch box and I was meant to take them. But the medication reduced my appetite. I would not eat my lunch and not take my tablets. This was a real problem for me because I always played up at the end of the day. A lot of schools demand that ADD/ADHD students go to the office to take their medication. This is all right when your son is young, but it also makes him feel different and again reinforces his low self-esteem.

As your son gets older, I suggest that he should be responsible for taking his own medication. If he does not take it, he will hurt himself. I also don't like the idea of an eighteen-year-old student going off to take his medication like a little kid. Come on, we are talking about adults.

The other problem I have is determining exactly when the medication has worn off. Just because it's lunchtime does this mean that all the children on these drugs are ready for their next dose? All children are different. I don't have the answer to this question.

How to Choose the Right School for Your Child

The right or wrong school can be the determining factor in the level of success your child achieves in both school and in life. If my parents hadn't chosen the right schools, I would not have succeeded. The right school will help your child resolve many of the problems caused by ADD/ADHD.

To choose the right school you must first know what makes a school good for an ADD/ADHD student. The first thing you need to look at is its size. I suggest the smallest school possible, with small classes. This will allow your child to have more one-on-one teaching. This is essential if your child is having trouble academically. The smaller classes also have a more settled working environment. This will help your child's concentration. In small schools the teachers often have more time to give to each student and there is a more caring environment.

Once you have found a small school, I suggest asking about any special education programs. Just come straight out and say it: "Does your school and do your teachers have any experience in dealing with ADD/ADHD students?" If they do, ask them for specifics. Find out about their sports and drama programs. Your child can burn off his excess energy in sports or other extracurricular activities.

A good question is, Does your school offer any big brother (older student) programs? These are great for ADD/ADHD students. It offers them remedial coaching with one-on-one teaching. It is amazing how much an ADD/ADHD student will listen to an older student. The next thing you want to find out is how many male teachers the school has. This may sound extremely sexist, but in my experience male ADD/ADHD students relate best to male teachers because they can handle a lot more boisterous behavior.

For ADD/ADHD children I believe the best types of schools are same-sex religious schools only because they have a higher standard of discipline and your child will need plenty of discipline to keep his behavior under control. State schools are hampered when some parents do not allow teachers to discipline their unruly children. I am not religious but my parents felt that a religious school would be the best and it would be right for me.

You must make a list of all the schools that you feel would be beneficial for your child. I strongly suggest that you take your son to all these schools on the list and let him decide. Then it is his decision and he can't turn around and blame you if he does not like the school.

For your son, try to get a male teacher. This may be hard, but do try.

A lot of ADD/ADHD students are made to repeat a year in their younger years. I think this is the worst thing you can do.

Sure, your child may be academically behind. But early on, who really cares? It will take years before your child catches up. The reason I don't like ADD/ADHD students being kept back is that it does so much harm to their self-confidence and causes further problems. You have to remember that your child is most probably extremely gifted in some area, like many ADD/ADHD people. But it takes years for an ADD/ADHD student to learn how to study in his own manner. We can concentrate—we just do it when we feel like it. So when your child realizes this, the results will astound both of you. Some of the greatest minds in history have shown many of the traits of ADD/ADHD. These people often had trouble in school, but when alone they could develop some remarkable results. According to Dr. Gordon Serfontein in his book *Attention Deficit Disorder in Adults* (Sydney: Simon & Schuster Australia, 1994), Albert Einstein had every ADD symptom under the sun.

What to Do If the School Has Had Enough of Your Child

Well, this is definitely my forte because I went to six schools. About every two years I had to find another school. Some parents often have real trouble with their child changing schools a lot. But it is not a real problem. It can be beneficial. As they say, a change is as good as a holiday. But what do you do when the school has had enough? In most cases you can't do a lot. You can try asking: "What is going to happen to my son if you expel him? Are you just going to move the problem on? I thought schools are meant to care about the youth of this country. Well, I guess I was wrong."

The only thing that really matters is that your son is happy at school. If he is upset just pull him out. Try, try, try again. If he is not going to make it at school, home schooling is always an option. Tutors are also great because your son can catch up working at home in a more stable environment. The one thing parents must realize is that not all kids will end up being rocket scientists. If your son is not going to make it academically, when appropriate, ask him if he would like to try a trade school or maybe an apprenticeship. He may be better at manual skills than academic theory. It's worth a try. As long as he is happy, who really cares? Not everyone can go or wants to go to college.

Relationships

Parents

Parents are at the center of an ADD/ADHD child's life. And the most important thing to understand is that it does not matter how much your child abuses you, he still loves you. I have already explained why parents often get the abuse and violence directed at them.

In my case, I know I would not have achieved anything in life without my mother. Thanks, Mum! My mother did everything for me. It's why this relationship is so important! My mum was the stabilizer of my family and she had a calming effect on me.

It's important for both parents to share the work of raising an ADD/ADHD child. If one parent isn't involved, it makes it really hard for the other.

If one parent is working and the other stays at home, the same problem arises time and time again at the end of the day.

When, for example, the father gets home from a long day at work, the last thing he wants to hear is, "Our son did this and did that." The son is often excited about his dad being home and wants to play. The father often shuts all this out and leaves it to his wife to cope. The father then stays at work later and later so he does not have to deal with it. This puts massive strain on the marriage, and many ADD/ADHD children's parents break up due to this constant pressure. I cannot stress how important it is for both parents to make an effort with their sons.

Siblings

This is a very hard relationship for both the siblings and the ADD/ADHD child. ADD/ADHD children are prone to annoy and frustrate their brothers and sisters. It is even worse when they go to the same school. The siblings are often associated with the bad things their brother (or sister) has done. In addition, the ADD/ADHD child often gets most of the attention from the parents. This makes it extremely hard on the siblings because they resent and are often jealous of the special treatment the ADD/ADHD child gets. This is what happened with my sister. She hated that I received so much special attention. To her it seemed unfair.

I suggest that you explain to your other children what is wrong with their sibling. This is all about understanding and awareness, and when people understand that ADD/ADHD children can't help the way they behave, a lot of the stigma about being the sibling of a bad kid is wiped away.

Family meetings are a good way to resolve issues that would

often otherwise end up in fights. You can't make your children like each other, but you can reduce the tension.

Another great idea is to ask an older cousin or a friend's older child—one your child looks up to—to spend time with your son. Children mimic the behavior of older kids, and this can be a good way to show your child the right way to behave. Getting an older child to tutor your child can be very beneficial, too.

Teachers

This relationship can be very beneficial for your child. It is of the utmost importance to explain to your son's teacher why he acts the way he does. This will give your son more of a chance to bend the rules without getting into trouble. The most important thing about a good student-teacher relationship is mutual respect. If your son hates his teacher, he will do everything in his power to annoy the teacher. But if your son likes his teacher, the teacher will be able to control your son better because he will see the teacher as a friend. In sixth year my coordinator always wondered why I never got into trouble in economics but was in trouble in every other class. I told her that it was simple. I liked the teacher and if he asked me to be quiet or do my work I would, because I didn't want to disappoint him. But I didn't like the other teachers as much, so I went out of my way to highlight this through disruptive behavior.

It is important for parents to establish good relationships with their child's teachers. A couple of chats a week will help you understand both the teacher's responsibility and your child's. It is great to find out what work is due.

Lazy Child!

I am constantly being told by my parents, "You don't do anything. You're so lazy, Ben!" This is a common trait in ADD/ADHD people. It contradicts the name attention deficit hyperactivity disorder. If I am meant to be hyperactive, how can I be lazy? It is not that we are deliberately lazy, we just have short bursts of energetic behavior. This is then followed by many hours, even days, of complete nothingness. It is not uncommon for me to study for twelve hours straight, then do nothing for days and lie in bed. It seems as if there can't be a mixture of the two.

Being lazy is a condition of ADD/ADHD people because they have so many thoughts and ideas it's hard for them to finish anything. Therefore, it seems as if nothing ever gets done! People with ADD/ADHD do not choose to be lazy, they just cannot concentrate on one thing at a time. They are constantly trying to will themselves to do things. But they just can't motivate themselves to do it.

How to Teach an ADD/ADHD Child

This is a huge problem for parents of children who have ADD/ADHD. How can you teach a child who can't concentrate and is not interested in the subject being taught? I believe that the problem with many ADD/ADHD children is not that they do not want to learn, because many ADD/ADHD children are hungry to gain knowledge. But the way they are taught is not appropriate for their learning style. Many parents spend thousands of dollars on learning aids to help their children, but these often don't work because they were developed for normal children. This problem arises again in the classroom. Teachers often have no idea how to teach an ADD/ADHD child. It does not matter how much you try to teach an ADD/ADHD child in the normal teaching style, he will gain little or nothing. This took me many years to understand, but when I did, I could teach myself.

So How Do ADD/ADHD Students Learn?

The first thing we must look at is why the old style of teaching is not appropriate for ADD/ADHD children. The problem with the old style is that it does not capture the imagination and the low concentration of ADD/ADHD students. How can you expect to teach a child math when it means nothing to him? What I am saying here is that when you open a math textbook it is full of numbers. It means nothing to an ADD/ADHD child. Conversely, a normal child is told that he must do the problems and hand in his homework the following day. He can do this because he does not have a problem with concentration and repetitive tasks.

It is the same problem with reading. I recently gave a talk to a group of ADD/ADHD second years who were failing at school. I asked them, "Who likes to read books?" Not one said he did. I asked why. They said, "Because it is boring," and some said they couldn't read anyway. I related to this predicament so well. I have a thirst for knowledge, but the only way you can get a good knowledge of a topic is to read many accounts of the topic. This was always a problem for me.

How to Teach ADD/ADHD Students to Enjoy Reading

It was only a few months ago that I read my first book cover to cover. While reading this book it occurred to me why I could not concentrate when reading books. It was not that I did not find the material interesting. It was that I was just reading words. If you pick up a book written in another language, it is just a bunch of paper with symbols on it. That is the problem that ADD/ADHD people have with books. When I was younger I complained that I read a couple of pages and then forgot what I had read. How could I understand a story if I could only remember 5 percent of it? Talking to other ADD/ADHD people, I learned they felt the same way.

The only way an ADD/ADHD student can read for long periods of time is by forgetting that he is reading words. The best way to do this is to become part of the book. I suggest choosing a character and becoming that character throughout the novel. Instead of reading a book, you are now experiencing and living the book. Instead of reading the book and the book telling you what you are thinking, you must think outside the book. It is like having your own movie screen in your mind. When your character chooses to do something in the novel, you must visualize the scene in your mind. Then ask yourself what you would do in the same situation.

There are a number of books on the market for teenage readers in which you choose your own destiny—you decide which way you will go in the story. How it works is that at the end of each chapter, you have the chance to choose from three scenarios. You then flip to whichever page you want and continue reading. These books are excellent because you must become a part of the book without actually having to use my technique. The only problem with these books is that at times they can become a little confusing to understand when you are constantly flipping pages. Overall, these books can be very useful.

How to Teach Young ADD/ADHD Students to Read

This is a major problem for both parents of and students who have ADD/ADHD. The problem with teaching young ADD/ADHD students is that they have short-term memory problems. I often become annoyed when trying to teach young ADD/ADHD students to read. One minute they can read a word, then the next minute they have forgotten it.

To teach an ADD/ADHD child to learn the first one hundred words or so of the English language is the most important thing. However, these words are often the hardest to read. For example, it is extremely hard to teach an ADD/ADHD child how to read the word "what" because when you say the word it sounds like it is spelled "wot." Most children can learn to read the first one hundred words of the English language by continually repeating and writing the words over and over, but this is not possible with an ADD/ADHD student. Once an ADD/ADHD child has read the word, he does not want to continually read and spell the word so that it is firmly stuck in his mind.

You must develop your own techniques for teaching an ADD/ADHD student to read. For example, if your child is interested in basketball you can play the game Horse. This is an excellent game for fathers to play with their sons. The way it works is, each time you make a shot, you get a letter. So if you make your first shot, you receive the letter H, and as you make shots you get more letters, until you have spelled the word "horse." You can then do this with other words such as "what," "where," "who," "the," "that," and so on. If learning is made fun, your child will want to learn. If you try to force your child to learn, you will have little success.

The learning technique can also be used when teaching math. You pick a sport such as football, baseball, basketball, and so on, depending on your child's interests, then you ask your son to do computations based on homeruns, batting statistics, or whatever else may interest him. These simple mathematical problems are extremely useful for your son when he is faced with the same problems in the classroom.

You can also try to make your son count his own running score of hits. This will help with his short-term memory and learning retention. These sums should also be done during and after the game. This will teach him to think ahead and plan for the future, something that is very hard for ADD/ADHD kids to do.

Once your young ADD/ADHD child has learned to read the first one hundred words of the English language, it is now time for him to start to put these into sentences. The same techniques used in playing Horse can also be used in the same way. The child will have to make sentences instead of spelling words. Once he can make sentences, it is time for him to read books. This will be tough to do. But with modification it should be much easier. The best way to do this is to find books that your son is interested in, for example on sports, music, cars, and so on. If he has trouble keeping an interest in books, you could use another source. When I was learning to read I hated reading books. However, I was very interested in Teenage Mutant Ninja Turtles, a fad then. My parents bought me Ninja Turtle trading cards. These cards have short stories and pictures on both the front and the back. I read the backs of the cards instead of books. They captured my short attention span.

Another modification that I suggest is visual reading. You find a book that your son is interested in and change it slightly. This may be very time-consuming but it is very effective. You will need to go out and buy a CD-ROM that has clip art on it. You can also download public domain pictures from the Internet. You will then need to retype the story on your computer. But every five to ten words instead of putting in the word, insert a picture of the thing the word represents. Then type the word under the picture. For example, place the words "fire engine" under a picture of a fire engine. This technique works in the same way as adapting a character in a novel. It is all about visual learning and stimulation.

Another modification is to color code word groups, for example "cat," "bat," "that," "mat," and so on. But color code only the "at" sound. If you do this in a number of books your son will visually learn the words. Flash cards with the first one hundred words on them using color coding are also a good tool. The problem is people use these flash cards in the wrong way. Many parents stick these cards on walls, doors, and so on. They then ask their son to read the cards, but this is impossible. How can they expect their son to read the words when there are another ninety-nine cards distracting his concentration? The flash cards should be used in another way. You should hold the cards right up in the face of your son. This way the only thing he will be able to concentrate on is that specific word. Then get your son to read that card. Because the cards are color coded he will again associate the color of the word with the sound. This will work at the start, but once your son can read most of the words he will become bored. The best way to resolve this problem is to use sports heroes and silly words and stories. By placing pictures of sports heroes, cars, and so on it again creates visual interest for your son. Once your son can read most of the words it is time to use words that will create interest, even if it's a rude or "dirty" word, such as "ass." You will be surprised at how much interest a seven-year-old will have when he reads the word "ass."

Telling stories with these flash cards is a fantastic way of retaining his interest. All you need to do is ask your son to read the word and then put that word into a story. He then chooses the next word and puts it into the story. It is a good idea to make the story involve your son and a sports hero and silly words. He will be constantly laughing and will want more and more. He won't even notice that he is learning.

Short-Term Memory Modifications

The game Concentration is an excellent way to improve short-term memory. You place playing cards facedown and try to find matching pairs. It is a very simple game but works very well. This should be played frequently with younger children because it is of the utmost importance to improve their short-term memory.

Many people—including teachers—have been astounded by my incredible long-term memory. But at the same time they cannot understand my poor short-term memory. This is a huge problem for me when trying to cram for exams. For many months I thought about why I have such a good long-term memory, and then it hit me. I don't remember isolated facts but I remember features of stories that I find amusing or interesting. For example, if I had to remember the date August 6, 1945, when the Allies dropped the atomic bombs on Japan, I would not have a chance in hell. But what I do is picture in my mind the massive mushroom cloud over Hiroshima. Then I visualize the date "August 6, 1945" being exploded instead. So when I need to remember the date all I need to do is visualize the mushroom cloud and the date pops into my head.

Another example is trying to teach an ADD/ADHD child to spell the word "surf." This is very hard to explain to an ADD/ADHD child and is most useful when he is around twelve. To remember how to spell the word "surf" you must visualize yourself surfing on the perfect wave. But just then a huge S on a surfboard cuts you off. U, R, F are surfing past as well, so follow them. When your son needs to remember how to spell "surf" all he needs to do is jump on his imaginary surfboard and the word will suddenly pop into his head.

I understand that this is very hard to explain to a child and even to some adults. But once you have mastered this memory technique you will be astounded by your new memory. It works by visually triggering a subtle cue in your mind. I think of my memory as being a bit like my room. I know that my keys are in it somewhere but I can't remember where. We have all looked for something and been unable to find it. But suddenly you remember something and it triggers your memory of where you put it. That is how this technique works. It allows you to remember strange and funny things and to remember boring things like dates and numbers.

Homework

Homework is one of the hardest things to try to get an ADD/ADHD student to do. I have always hated doing homework. In fact, I never did any substantial homework until I got to sixth year. It was during this period that I learned a lot more about myself and how my brain works. I have already discussed how I do my homework but that may not work for everyone! Here are some ideas for helping your child do homework on a regular basis.

First, keep on top of what is due and when. ADD/ADHD students often forget about homework and due dates. Once you have found out what is due and when, you should make a huge sign in your child's room to give him a constant reminder of the tasks ahead. Once the work is done, get your child to cross the task off and give him a reward for completing the homework on time.

And most important, you must make homework fun. Do not make it a chore or a punishment. Encourage your son to want to learn. Motivate him. First, all subjects must be organized into color-coded folders, English in red, history in blue, and so on. Each folder should have a picture of a favorite sports star or hero on the front. When your son gets older, pictures of models and movie stars can be used. Homework must be done at the same time every night and start and finish at the same time. When it is time to do homework instead of saying, "Get your red English homework folder," you should say "Get your Michael Jordan folder." This takes away some of the negativity of doing homework from the start. Along with this, you can use bribery and treats to motivate, for example, sticking treats on the folder. This again makes doing homework enjoyable.

Trying to make an ADD/ADHD student do something he is not mentally ready to do is very hard. Most people don't understand that sometimes an ADD/ADHD person can be perfectly capable of doing homework and the next day he can't concentrate on the simplest tasks. This is a common problem for me. Some days I am lazy and can't move. But then the next day I am so hyper I can't sit still. When something needs to be done like homework, I can't mentally do it. I can't concentrate.

I have overcome this problem with exercise and active behavior. If I feel that I am too hyper and can't sit still, I go and do something energetic before I sit down and do homework. This feeling of hyperactivity often comes back when doing homework, and when I feel it coming on, I know that it is time to do something energetic. I often just get up and walk out of my room and go and swing a golf club. It takes only a couple of minutes, then I am fine and ready to study again. This was a problem in class because I could not just walk out and go swing a golf club! Parents and teachers need to be aware of this and let the ADD/ADHD student walk off and come back in a couple of minutes. Teachers can do it subtly by getting the ADD/ADHD student to go and take a note to another teacher on the other side of the school. All the note needs to say is that so and so needs a break.

When I was in sixth year, my mother bought a straw hat from a charity shop for a fancy-dress party. This hat became my homework hat that year. Every time I started homework, I put the hat on. This visual cue told my brain that it was time to do homework. When I stopped or when I went outside to swing the golf club, the hat came off. I still have the hat today, but it is destroyed because I threw it across the room when I was sick of doing homework. I plan to keep it forever.

Another excellent aid for ADD/ADHD students is the personal computer. If I did not have a computer, I would not have achieved anything. ADD/ADHD children often have many problems with spelling and writing. The computer helps. Spell check is the greatest thing invented. A word-processing program is even better. It allows an ADD/ADHD person to express his ideas and thoughts so other people can read them. If I had written this book with a pen, I couldn't have even read my own writing, and I guess my editor would have had no chance.

The computer is most useful for ADD/ADHD people when it is away from the family. It allows an ADD/ADHD child to work quietly without distractions. For parents, it is also useful as an escape and a learning aid. The Internet often attracts ADD/ADHD people because it allows them to absorb lots of different information. When they are bored or not interested in that topic anymore all they need to do is find something else. The computer can also help with schoolwork. There are heaps of good learning games on the market that provide visual stimulation and in which the challenge increases with ability. Most are made for use by one person. The computer becomes an ADD/ADHD person's own personal tutor.

The other thing about homework is that parents and students should discuss with their teachers if it is possible to choose the topic of the assignment. This can be very useful for ADD/ADHD students because if they pick the topics, they will be much more interested in the work. Some teachers will not like this idea, but try to convince them. In my opinion, it does not matter what your son learns as long as he is learning something. Once he is older and understands how his own mind works, he will be able to tackle even uninteresting material. But it is very important for younger ADD/ADHD students to learn something about anything.

ADD/ADHD Jobs and Careers

People with ADD/ADHD often find themselves either hating their jobs or changing jobs all the time. Statistics show that ADD/ADHD people change jobs three times more often than the average person. This is a result of being easily bored and un-stimulated in the workplace. I am constantly swapping part-time jobs because I either get bored and play up and get fired or I quit. My biggest problem is that I do not respond well to au-thority figures. This is not a good trait when you are sixteen and tell your boss that he is stupid. But that's me!

A few years ago I decided, or realized, that I was not going to be able to work for anyone but myself, as a result of my problem with authority and thinking most bosses are stupid. They're not, but I can't handle being told what to do. Therefore I decided that I should stop doing courses for a bachelor of business ad-ministration and start studying for a bachelor of business in en-trepreneurial studies. My theory is that if I am going to be fired, it is better to fire myself.

However, this is not appropriate in all cases. So I have suggested some jobs that I think are a good fit for ADD/ADHD people. Obviously there are many other suitable jobs. The most unsuitable is any job that is repetitive and/or boring. The ADD/ADHD person will not stay in a boring job. The key in all these careers is constant stimulation and excitement. But more important, they allow ADD/ADHD people to work by themselves without being restricted by their employers.

author
professional athlete
computer technology specialist
real estate agent
stockbroker
plumber
builder
electrician
actor
entrepreneur
soldier
police officer
firefighter
advertising representative
politician

Sex

ADD/ADHD people are at greater risk of contracting sexually transmitted diseases compared to the normal population. This is a result of having sex without using protection. ADD/ADHD people are sometimes described as sex maniacs. But this is a huge generalization. I believe that the reason some ADD/ADHD people like to have sex a lot is because it's exciting.

However, the problem still remains that ADD/ADHD people are more likely to contract sexually transmitted diseases than the norm. Also, teenage pregnancy is an issue for ADD/ADHD girls. Along with this, ADD/ADHD people often abuse alcohol and drugs. This also places them in danger of having unprotected sex.

Parents, you must realize that your children are going to have sex and you can't stop them. But you must do all you can to protect your children. Sex education at school is not enough. Parents must take an active role and explain the risks of and the alternatives to unprotected sex.

Interesting Statistics About ADD/ADHD Adolescents*

ADD/ADHD adolescents

- begin sexual activity one year earlier (at 14–15 years)
- have more sexual partners and spend less time with each
- are less likely to employ contraception
- have teen pregnancies (38 percent versus 4 percent)
- usually do not have custody of offspring (54 percent)
- are treated for STDs (16 percent versus 4 percent)
- use alcohol and marijuana more
- are at greater risk for cardiovascular disease

I asked a doctor why ADD/ADHD people are at risk for cardiovascular disease. He told me that it was because our hearts beat more because we are always on the go—meaning we live a very stressful life. I said to him I believed that it was due to all the other statistics mentioned. He laughed and said that might be the case, too!

*From *Proceedings of the ADHD in the Third Millennium Conference* (Westmead Hospital, Sydney, Australia, March 16–18, 2001), p. 98.

Other ADD/ADHD Challenges

Obsessions and Fads

Obsessions and fads are very common in ADD/ADHD people. Fads can often drive parents crazy—having to be constantly told about something until they, too, are experts in that field. I personally put my parents through the Teenage Mutant Ninja Turtles University until I got over it around four years later. Obsessions are even more annoying to parents—for example, their child becoming fixated with disliking a teacher or a relative. I don't think that it is often the actual person or television program that causes the obsession. Instead, it is the excitement and feeling of aliveness that young ADD/ADHD people get when their obsession or fad is discussed.

Parents should not try to prevent these fads and obsessions. They can be very useful tools in the classroom. Instead of viewing them as a disadvantage, use them. See if you can involve your child's fad in everyday life as much as possible when it comes to getting him to do boring tasks such as homework, cleaning his room, etc. He will show more interest if his fad or obsession is linked directly to the unstimulating tasks.

Impulsivity

Being an impulsive person can get you into a lot of trouble—as you have already seen with my life. However, I feel that impulsivity is the best gift I have been given. People have always tried to discourage my impulsiveness. But I think we should embrace and encourage impulsiveness in ADD/ADHD people. Since they can't get rid of it, they might as well use it to their advantage. If the child wants to do something (and it's not dangerous), let him go ahead and do it. ADD/ADHD people learn from their mistakes. If they want to pull their bike to bits, let them do it. This may lead to them having interests in other areas—such as walking!

A large percentage of important discoveries were made by people with traits such as you find in ADD/ADHD people. So let your son be impulsive and explore the world!

Social Difficulties

ADD/ADHD people commonly have social difficulties, not only when growing up but throughout their lives. If you think differently than the norm, you therefore act differently. ADD/ADHD people often have many jobs because they get bored, and they get fired from their position. ADD/ADHD people *do* have a place in society, but it takes years for them to find it; many find it in places you wouldn't even think of. There are high levels of ADD/ADHD people in the police force and armed forces because these positions promote a structured environment, and ADD/ADHD adults work well in a structured environment.

But these social problems are a real concern because these abnormal behaviors can affect those around you, especially family members and siblings. I'm talking about ADD/ADHD adults now, not children. Think about your own relatives. Most probably there is someone in your family who fits the stereotype I have just painted. But these people don't mean to be as destructive as they can sometimes be.

Organizational Skills

All ADD/ADHD books will discuss organizational skills because it seems to be a major problem. ADD/ADHD people are disorganized.

Look, I will be honest. I am still very disorganized and I really can't see much changing. But a few simple things can make a difference. A diary should work, in theory, but ADD/ADHD students seem to use them for everything other than what they are intended for, such as drawing in or throwing at other kids. Parents should regularly check their son's diary and school bag for dates of assignments, and write extra reminders in the diary. Discuss time constraints with your child. Talk about how long the assignments should take. Because ADD/ADHD children are impulsive, time often means nothing to them. So if they want to go out with friends, you can remind them—not nag them—about the work that needs to be completed first.

It's all about helping them make sense of a very scattered life they live. Help them, but don't ask unrealistic things of them.

As they get older, they may find that voice diaries are very useful. ADD/ADHD people often hate writing because their handwriting is sloppy and they can't read it anyway. A voice recorder is great because they often love hearing their own voice.

Lessons from History

I once hated history and thought studying it was a waste of time. I didn't care what had happened before me. I am a now person—what was happening *now* was all that mattered. Then one day I asked my history teacher, "What do we need history for?" The reply was: "To predict the future, we must first understand the past!" It sounded good but I didn't quite understand it until I was much older. There is one certain thing on this planet and that is there has been nothing new. It has all happened before with a few variations. Countries, armies, leaders, diseases, miracles—all come and go. The same goes for people and especially ADD/ADHD people. What parents are dealing with now with their ADD/ADHD children has been happening for thousands of years. There are many famous people now suspected of having had ADD/ADHD. If you are interested, all you need to do is search for "famous ADD people" on the Internet. You will be surprised at first. Then when you think about them it will make a lot of sense. Therefore, I will discuss two famous ADD people. The interesting thing I have found in researching famous ADD people is that many of these people failed at school, but they succeeded in life. As already discussed, it's not easy for ADD people of today to succeed without a good education. The other interesting thing I have found is that these famous ADD people were all brilliant. But at the same time they would seem very mad and crazy to non-ADD people. As the saying goes, "It's a very fine line between brilliance and utter madness." This basically describes me to a T. My mother often says, "How can someone so intelligent be so stupid?"

The King of ADD: Winston Churchill

Dr. Serfontein's book *Attention Deficit Disorder in Adults* states that as a young boy, Winston Churchill showed all the characteristics of ADD. He was a very mischievous boy who was always in trouble and antagonizing people. Winston's mother often complained to his father about the way Winston constantly teased his younger brother. Winston said himself that he was "what grown-up people in their offhand way call a troublesome boy."

He had major problems at school, especially in his early school days. He was described as a daydreamer and could never stay on task. His schoolwork and homework were never completed on time and often not done at all. His poor attention in the classroom got him into a lot of trouble. He was disorganized and constantly late for class. His parents did not know what would happen to him and if he would amount to anything.

However, like many ADD people who show early signs of achieving little, he demonstrated to the world what can be achieved when you put your mind to it. When he finished school he joined the army and traveled the world. He fought in many wars and conflicts across the globe. He had many near-death experiences as a result of his impulsive and sometimes stupid behavior. He has been described as very brave. I suspect that it was not so much courage as impulsiveness. He didn't think about consequences—a common trait in ADD people. Many brave acts have been later described as completely crazy and stupid. Brave people often realize afterward how dangerous their behavior was. However, the fact still remains that Churchill performed some very brave deeds and he should be respected and honored for them.

In his army days, Churchill recognized his fascination and ability as a writer and more important as a speechmaker. When he left the army, he followed his abilities in these fields and became one of the greatest politicians the world has ever seen. Like many ADD people, he had an ability to grasp very complex problems quickly. This was one of his major strengths when leading the Allies to victory against the Nazis. When Churchill was handed long reports on the war, he was not able to concentrate enough to read all the pages. Therefore, he was given simplified one- to two-page reports—what we know today as an executive summary. What was more important than Churchill's ability to grasp impossible concepts in a matter of minutes was his ability to translate and communicate them to the general public.

His impulsive nature and ability to understand complex problems was a key factor in defeating the Germans. He was able to understand a problem and then act upon it as soon as possible.

This impulsiveness sometimes ended in horrific disaster, especially during the war. But most of the time it was dramatically successful.

The one thing that made Churchill such a success was not his family or even his ADD—it was that he learned to control his erratic behavior. In his childhood and early twenties, he was in a restrictive environment—school and the army. ADD people need routine, and the institutions Churchill attended were based on routine. Later in life, he adopted these skills himself. Without this early training, I do not feel he would have been such a success.

Albert Einstein

Dr. Serfontein also believes Albert Einstein had ADD. Einstein was best known for his theory of relativity. But he was also respected as the founder of contemporary science and physics theory. His theories are still fundamentally important to today's scientific approaches. The later development of the atomic bomb can also be attributed to his research, although he disagreed with its development and use. When Einstein was twelve he came to believe that God did not exist. This allowed him to free himself from the spiritual and ethical restrictions of being a believer. As a young boy, Einstein had learning difficulties. At age four he could speak only two-word sentences. As a result of his late development, he was believed to be mentally retarded. His tremendous difficulties at school were attributed to his poor concentration. In class he was always distracted, thinking about things other than what was being taught. The two things he could concentrate on, though, were arithmetic and science.

Einstein dropped out of school but continued to study on his own. When his father's business failed, he had to find employment and support himself. Einstein thought that he would excel at electrical engineering and applied to study at the Swiss Polytechnic before he finished high school, but he failed the general entrance exam. However, he scored very high on the mathematics section, and the school suggested that he work for a diploma at a Swiss high school and reapply. He did and was accepted the following year.

Like Winston Churchill, Albert Einstein's true ability was to break down complex problems into smaller parts. This is how he solved some of modern man's most complex mathematical and scientific equations.

Einstein was not an angry and violent ADD person, as can be the case with some ADD people. He was more of the inattentive and easily distracted type. Einstein's success, like Winston Churchill's, was due to his being able to control his concentration through a deliberate and ordered life. Similar to his ability to disregard the clutter of mathematical problems and reach the core of the problem, Einstein was able to free his mind of clutter and concentrate on his research and studies.

Conclusion

Join the System, Don't Fight It!

This is what I try to teach all ADD/ADHD adolescents with whom I come in contact. They often feel isolated and become alienated by society. So they do what most oppressed people do: They rebel against society. But what they don't realize is that they can't win—not in school nor in life in general. ADD/ADHD kids often believe they can and will beat authority. And often they realize too late—when they have been kicked out of school or thrown in jail—that they can't. I hate seeing kids with this attitude, because this is what I believed when I was younger. It wasn't until I was seventeen that I realized I had to work with the system, if I wanted to get what I wanted!

So work the system, kids. If you can't beat them join them!

The Differences That Make the Difference

Okay, so why do some ADD/ADHD kids make it and others don't? Well, that seems like a very hard question, but it's not. The first thing is love, and lots of it. Especially from parents and family and, more important, from oneself, which can come only from self-respect and feelings of being wanted and needed. This comes from the family.

The second thing is support from both the family and the school. This is very important because parents must work with the school in providing support.

The third thing is a desire to be a better person. But this needs self-belief, and that can only be developed from achievement. So give your son a chance and let him live. If he falls, pick him up and encourage him to have another go.

The fourth thing is a good doctor who wants to help your child. If you're not having any results with your current doctor, find another one. Ask lots of questions. People, for some reason, see doctors as some sort of higher humans who know everything. Patients tend not to ask questions or demand answers.

The fifth thing is a really understanding grandparent to dump your son on, when you need a break! But, on a serious note, being caring and understanding is fundamental.

ADD/ADHD: It's Just a State of Mind

If you go through your whole life thinking you can't do something, you won't try it. I feel that many ADD/ADHD people have been so burned by life that they give up trying anymore. Failing is a horrible feeling.

But I hate the fact that people look at ADD/ADHD and other disorders as an easy way out. Parents and teachers often blame everything on their son having ADD/ADHD. That is wrong!

Once you master your own ADD/ADHD and realize that it's just a state of mind, you can do anything you put your mind to: learn the skills you lack and work on the ones you have.

Well, I say play the hand you've been dealt and put on your best poker face and bluff the table and get on with life.

And Finally . . .

Writing this book is my greatest achievement to date. It took many long months to write. I hope that all my hard work will help other people to understand ADD/ADHD—and more important, their children—better. Always keep in mind that the only way for your child to survive in this world is through hard work. A parent's love and understanding is the greatest gift you can give your child. Along with this, patience and an open mind will help your family function in a more normal manner.

If I had not had my strong family support I would have not achieved anything. I would have ended up just another statistic, a juvenile ADD/ADHD person in jail.

Hope is the best gift I can give parents and children with ADD/ADHD. I have severe ADHD, but my parents and I never gave up and I finally made it through school. Now I am an internationally published author and I hate books! Who would have thought that a person with a diagnosed mental and learning disability would make it to these heights? Most people don't know that I can't spell properly, let alone read my own handwriting. I lack other skills too, but I have learned to work around them. It sounds absurd that a person who can't spell can write a book, but I have. But what sounds even more ridiculous is someone writing a book who has only ever read one book cover to cover before. But I did. I am not trying to boast. I am just stating that anything is possible if you put your mind to it!

On a closing note, I would like to thank everyone who purchased and read my book. If you got this far, you obviously thought it was worth reading. I hope that you now understand ADD/ADHD and your child better than before you read it. I wish you and your child the greatest success in this sometimes crazy world.

Always remember to reach for the stars!

About the Author

Benjamin Polis self-published his book with great success in his native Australia and now lectures internationally on ADD/ADHD.